YEATS' IRELAND

Yeats' Ireland

an illustrated anthology

Benedict Kiely

AURUM PRESS

First published 1989 by Aurum Press Limited
33 Museum Street, London WC1A 1LD

Reprinted 1990

W. B. Yeats extracts copyright © by Michael B. Yeats
Editorial content copyright © 1989 by Benedict Kiely
Design copyright © 1989 by Aurum Press Ltd

British Library Cataloguing in Publication Data

Yeats, W.B. (William Butler), *1865–1939*
    Yeats' Ireland.
    I. Title   II. Kiely, Benedict, *1919–*
    821'.8

ISBN 1 85410 014 9

(Frontispiece) 'To an Isle in the Water...'
Derry Clare Lough, County Galway.

Picture research by Juliet Brightmore
Designed by Derek Birdsall RDI

Typeset by August Filmsetting, Haydock, St Helens
Printed in Italy by Lego Spa

CONTENTS

INTRODUCTION

In the summer of 1906 John Butler Yeats, a most remarkable man and father, wrote to his son William, then forty-one years of age, one of his many quite wonderful letters. His subjects were Mrs Patrick Campbell, the great actress, our own classical heroine, Deirdre of the Sorrows, and the tragic play that William had just completed about that poor queen who had, according to the poet, James Stephens, become only a story that can be told beside the fire: 'No man can ever be the friend of that poor queen.' Stephens in a prose romance, William Butler Yeats, A.E. (George Russell) and John Synge in stage plays, and others in other ways, had all paid their respects to the tragedy of Deirdre and the sons of Uisneach.

John B. Yeats wondered, when he wrote, whether or not Mrs Patrick Campbell should play the part of Deirdre in William's tragedy and, after that, he had a few words to say about the relationship between William and the country in which he had been born. But let John Butler Yeats speak for himself. He was always well able to do so.

The poet tells us that as a boy he had, and rode, a red pony. His brother, Jack, may here have celebrated that same pony.

My dear Willie — What are you going to do about Mrs Pat Campbell? I think it is a difficult question. No doubt the ideal thing is to keep the play for the Irish theatre, and we all and you especially ought to do ideal things — it might also be the prudent thing. The theatre is a very serious product of the Irish National Movement, we are all embarked in it — giving it your best play will give you a considerable accession of fortune, and authority with such people as John Quinn, and besides all this, it is the dignified thing to do.

In giving it to Mrs P. Campbell or any other famous personage, there is nothing very significant. It would simply be a piece of self-interest, which of course is a very good thing in its way, and especially in your case, who being a poet suffer much from lack of pence.

Only I think whatever you do it should not be done hastily, and you should not forget that you are a public man in the Irish movement — and its leader in all literary and philosophical movements and that your influence here is really more important to you than anything else, and dearer to you — and more important than anything else to other people as well.

Now there was a wise father speaking to a man who, as the father was always aware, was a most unusual son. (John Quinn was, as we all know, the rich American, and generous patron of the arts in relation to all things Irish.)

A man's country begins, in the vast generality of cases – and that qualification is not made with either levity or irony – with his father and mother: nor would it be any waste of time or space to consider for a while a few more of the words of John Butler Yeats. Certainly the most notable of all those words were those in which he revealed how conscious he was that when he married into the Pollexfen family and begot children, he had, as he said, given a tongue to the sea-cliffs. The Pollexfens of Sligo, merchants and millers and men of the sea and the ships, were strong men but silent, it would seem. John Yeats commented, 'Inarticulate as the sea-cliffs were the Pollexfens, lying buried under mountains of silence. They were released from bondage by contact with the joyous amiability of my family, and of my bringing up, and so all my four children are articulate, and yet with the Pollexfen force.'

George Pollexfen, whose sister he was to marry, met John Yeats when the two of them were schoolboys at the Atholl Academy, which was kept by a Scotsman on the Isle of Man. One does not have to be a firm believer in astrology, stars in their courses set and every wandering star, to feel that over that meeting bright stars shone. The Yeats family already had a connection with Sligo, at Drumcliff where, we have been firmly told, an ancestor was rector there long years ago. But the Yeats and Pollexfen connection that began, auspic-iously, on the Celtic Island of Mananaan Mac Lir, made it certain that the Ireland of William Butler Yeats began in an enchanted, western place by one of the most beautiful of Ireland's lakes and between two sacred mountains: Knocknarea, which is still the throne of Queen Maeve of Connacht, and Ben Bulben, of Fionn and the tragic legend of the death of Diarmuid.

In that place Yeats' mythologies had their origins and, later, after his momentous meeting with Augusta, Lady Gregory, underwent renewal and strengthening from the sacred fountains in the seven woods of Coole, and by the tower of Ballylee and the crossroads of Kil-tartan. He wrote at the end of the last century, when he had lived somewhat less than half his life:

I must leave my myths and images to explain themselves as the years go by and one poem lights up another ... I would, if I could, add to that majestic heraldry of the poets, that great and complicated inheritance of images which written

A SPIRIT OR SIDHE IN A LANDSCAPE
by George Russell (1867–1935).
George Russell thought that the ancient gods might emerge from 'the great gates of the mountains'.
This could be his vision of Aoibheall, Queen of the ancient people.

literature has substituted for the greater and more complex inheritance of the spoken tradition, some new heraldic images gathered from the lips of the common people. Christianity and the old nature faiths have lain down side by side in the cottages, and I would proclaim that peace as loudly as I can among the Kingdoms of poetry, where there is no peace that is not joyous, no battle that does not give life instead of death.

He wrote of 'a subtlety of desire, an emotion of sacrifice, a delight in order, that are perhaps Christian, and myths and images that mirror the energy of woods and streams and of their wild creatures'.

And he continued, 'Has any part of that majestic heraldry of the poets had a very different fountain? Is it not the ritual of the marriage of heaven and earth?'

Commenting on those words in her *W. B. Yeats: His Poetry and Thought*, Dr A. G. Stock said that they showed how deeply serious Yeats was about his mythological imagery even though, in 1899, he might not yet have been able to give a clear account of its meaning:

He was not merely playing with decorative language; the powers which he calls the 'energies of woods and streams and of their wild creatures' meant enough for him to set them up beside Christianity as a starting-point for an alternative interpretation of life. It was only a starting-point, for then and always he was too wise a poet to write down more doctrine than he could vitalize with poetry distilled from his inward experience ...

Elsewhere Yeats said, 'Have not all nations had their first unity from a mythology that marries them to rock and hill.'

That sentence comes back to me whenever I walk in the Sligo or the Coole countryside and wonder, at moments, which came first: the place or the poet? Once, by the lakes at Coole, I stood with an American friend, the late Kevin Sullivan, then Dean of Columbia University. The immortal swans were on the water. We counted them. Nine and fifty – the exact number mentioned, 'Upon the brimming water among the stones', in the poem. Since my friend was not the sort of American who carries a camera, he said sadly, 'No man or woman is ever going to believe this.' So I made a vow to retell that story on every suitable occasion.

'Some new heraldic images gathered from the lips of the common people ... ' And in relation to that

(Left) Father and son.

In 1917 Yeats married George Hyde-Lees.

*'May God be praised for woman
That gives up all her mind,
A man may find in no man
A friendship of her kind...'*
                    'On Woman'

national unity deriving from a mythology that married a culture to rock and hill, Yeats also said:

We had in Ireland imaginative stories, which the uneducated classes knew and even sang, and might we not make those stories current among the educated classes, rediscovering for the work's sake what I have called, 'the applied arts of literature', the association of literature, that is, with music, speech and dance, and at last, it might be, so deepen the political passion of the nation that all, artist and poet, craftsman and day-labourer would accept a common design?

That was a fine vision and it was shared, in varying degrees, by Douglas Hyde and Eoin MacNeill and others, and by most of the early enthusiasts of the Gaelic League, founded in 1893, who saw a cultural and, in some cases, a political necessity for the de-

Over the Bailey lighthouse, the northern sentinel of Dublin Bay, the poet saw the white birds flying.

Anglicization of Ireland. It must be noted that when Yeats spoke of uneducated classes and educated classes he was not, in the first instance, belittling nor, in the second, commending. It was merely a matter of what, and which, schools a person had attended, and for how long, and Yeats' views on the state of formal education in Ireland, and elsewhere, as well as on Catholic education in Ireland, could frequently be critical. Patrick Pearse, who kept his own Gaelicized school at St Enda's, and who rode his wingèd horse (and was to be executed in 1916 for other matters, and to be suitably mourned by poets and people), had described the system of British-controlled primary-education in Ireland as the Murder Machine. Few candid observers, then or since, could have faulted the description.

In the late 1880s and early 1890s Yeats put together, from printed sources, his collections of Irish folktales and stories from that other world of Ireland: the world of Faery or of the Good People. He was searching for his country and for his own consciousness along all those boreens, or lanes, of folktale and fairytale, and he found that the folklorist, Crofton Croker, who had stumbled through some of those ways and crossways before him, had been guilty of that 'great sin against art — the sin of rationalism. He tried to take away from his stories the impossibility that makes them dear to us.'

Thus, a long time before Daniel Corkery sharply noted in *Synge and Anglo-Irish Literature* that the novelists Charles Lever and Samuel Lover and others saw the Irish people as incapable of going much beyond the dictation of mother-wit, the young Mr Yeats wrote that

Croker and Lover, full of the ideas of the harum-scarum Irish gentility, saw everything humorized:

The impulse of the Irish literature of their time came from a class that did not — mainly for political reasons — take the populace seriously, and imagined the country as a humorist's Arcadia: its passion, its gloom, its tragedy, they knew nothing of. What they did was not wholly false; they merely magnified an irresponsible type, found oftenest among boatsmen, car men and gentlemen's servants, into the type of a whole nation, and created the stage Irishman.

He was, in a way, caught between the Ireland of the patriotic verse of Thomas Davis of the 1840s, the Ireland of John O'Leary, the Fenian of the 1860s (still a living and stimulating presence), and of that most inspirational creature, Maud Gonne; caught between all that and an ancient Ireland of the folk-imagination in which his spirit was easily at home. He stated his problems and his beliefs when he wrote the lines 'To Ireland in the Coming Times'. Elemental creatures go, he was convinced, about his table to and fro, and he said to himself that they were surely there, the divine people, for 'only we who have neither simplicity nor wisdom have denied them, and the simple of all times, and the wise men of ancient times have seen them and even spoken to them'.

In putting together those early anthologies of folklore and legend Yeats was seeking his symbols, and himself, as later he was to do in *The Celtic Twilight* and *The Secret Rose*, and in the higher and more complicated world of the *Saga of the Red Branch* and the story of Cuchulain battling to the death with the ungovernable sea. He was seeking not, perhaps, the meaning behind any mystery, but what he had already determined to find: a revelation of character, that 'of race and that of soul', a poetic and passionate gesture; seeking a world of the imagination far away from the spinning-jenny which the Almighty extracted from the side of Locke when the philosopher fell into a swoon and the garden died — a world that fed on dreaming and played not, like Tyndall and Thomas Huxley and the poet's own father, with the painted toy of grey truth.

But that 'very perceptive father had always told him that he was far too much in love with the world to find truth, as mystics do, by detaching himself from it'.

To the end of his days William Yeats could ask, 'What if the irrational should return?' The world we live in seems to have answered his question in a most unpleasant way. All of that he may have foreseen, not only in his later vision of the rough beast of 'The Second Coming', but in his early ideas on that rough, rug-headed Irish cousin of Puck of Pook's Hill, the night-riding Pooka.

Dr Mary Helen Thuente, in her book *W. B. Yeats and Irish Folklore*, draws our attention to the way in which Yeats radically altered the nature of that odd fellow. In the folklore material Yeats consulted, the Pooka appears as nothing worse than a mischievous prankster. Although, for myself, I must honestly confess that it has always puzzled me that a devil so gormless should pick for his abode that gloomy gorge where the road from Blessington to Baltinglass crosses the stripling River Liffey: Poulaphuca, Poulaphuca, the Pooka's Hole, a name that whispers mysteriously in *Finnegans Wake*.

Perhaps a view of that awesome place may have encouraged the young Yeats to consider that the Pooka was of the race of nightmare, an animal spirit living on solitary mountains and among old ruins, and 'grown monstrous with much solitude'. Perhaps the solitariness of the creature that could be now a horse, now an ass, now a bull, now a goat, now an eagle, was only a reflection of the mind of the young poet brooding among the bracken on Howth Head over Dublin Bay: 'Like all spirits he is only half in the world of form.'

As he wrote his very first poems, the world Yeats imagined was a retreat and, looking back on that time, he said later that his ideas of what a long poem should be were inspired by a thicket between three roads, some distance from any of them, in the midst of Howth:

That thicket gave me my first thought of what a long poem should be; I thought of it as a region into which one should wander from the cares of life. The characters were to be no more real than the shadows that people the Howth thicket. Their mission was to lessen the solitude without destroying its peace.

It was to be a long road, traversing many worlds, from that thicket above Dublin Bay back to Drumcliff churchyard by the western sea and under the bare head of Ben Bulben: and to his last will and testament to Irish poets. But in solitude, in the shadow of ancient Ireland, the young Yeats sought a simplicity that the nineteenth-century world of advancing industrialism seemed to deny. He quoted with approval the proverb that said that wisdom had alighted on three things: the hand of the Chinese, the brain of the Frank, and the tongue of the Arab. He believed that the most eloquent people on earth might be, as was once stated, the Arabs, who had only the bare earth of the desert and a sky swept bare by the sun. It must always be remembered that he was then a young man, writing the best part of a century ago, when England had the coal and iron and was master, or whatever, of the seven seas, and had the trust in material things that went with such dominance, and the Arabs had all the camels, and oil might as readily have been chrism. And these days of television, God help us, and the instant worldwide reporting of calamity give an added poignancy to this passage:

Those folktales are full of simplicity and musical occurrences for they are the literature of a class for whom every incident in the old rut of birth, love, pain and death has cropped up unchanged for centuries; who have steeped everything in the heart; to whom everything is a symbol. They have the spade over which man has leant from the beginning. The people of the cities have the machine, which is prose and a parvenu. They have few events. They can turn over the incidents of a long life as they sit by the fire. With us, nothing has time to father meaning, and too many things are occurring for even a big heart to hold ...

There is some ambiguity in identification there. But no matter. Anon, we will come, as the poet himself did, to the cities and their people.

John Butler Yeats, who had nothing if not high intellectual style and high notions, was, we are told, fond of saying that a gentleman is a gentleman simply because he has not 'the doctrine of *getting on* and the habit of it. The contest is not against material things, but between those who want and those who don't want to get on, having other important things to attend to.'

But money or the lack of it, and not just the mere and ungentlemanly desire to get on, drove or dragged him to London when the poet was nine years of age. This brought his rather remarkable family into that world of pre-Raphaelite dream, of Morris and Rossetti; and that world, particularly in the person and family, and prose and poetry, and crafts and artistic enterprises of William Morris, did have an influence – most considerable – on the poet and his brother and sisters. This was to be evidenced, in due time, in the Dun Emer Press and The Cuala Press, which would perhaps also explain the attachment of our poet to that most leisurely and mannered of prose-romances, *The Sundering Flood.*

But to the nervous, unhappy young boy from Sligo any benefits or delights to be derived from life in London were away in the future. At school there, he walked into a play-up-play-up-and-play-the-game world admired by, say, Henry Newbolt but heartily loathed even by Rudyard Kipling who had also suffered there. Yeats longed for Sligo and Memory Harbour and for the enchanted lake. He wrote most movingly:

A poignant memory came upon me the other day while I was passing the drinking-fountain near Holland Park, for there I and my sister had spoken together of our longing for Sligo and our hatred of London. I know we were both very close to tears and remember with wonder, for I had never known anyone that cared for such mementoes, that I longed for a sod of earth from some field I knew, something of Sligo to hold in my hand. It was some old race instinct like that of a savage, for we had been brought up to laugh at all displays of emotion. Yet it was our mother, who would have thought its display a vulgarity, who kept alive that love. She would spend hours listening to stories or telling stories of the pilots and fishing-people of Rosses Point, or of her own Sligo girlhood, and it was always assumed between her and us that Sligo was more beautiful than other places.

In that strange, slow-moving novel of his, *John Sherman*, Yeats gives the fullest account of the slight happening that led to the early lyric poem, 'The Lake Isle of Innisfree', which, for better or worse, has been the introduction for most of us to William Butler Yeats:

Delayed by a crush in The Strand, he heard a faint trickling of water nearby; it came from a shop-window where a little water-jet balanced a wooden ball upon its point. The sound suggested a cataract with a long Gaelic name, that leaped crying into the gate of the winds at Ballagh ...
He was set dreaming a whole day by walking down one Sunday morning to the borders of the Thames, a few hundred yards from his house – and looking at the osier-covered Chiswick Eyot. It made him remember an old day-dream of his. The source of the river that passed his garden at home was a certain wood-bordered and islanded lake, whither in childhood he had often gone blackberrying. At the further end was a little islet called Innisfree. Its rocky centre,

covered with many bushes, rose some forty feet above the lake. Often when life and its difficulties had seemed to him like the lessons of some older boy given to a younger by mistake, it had seemed good to dream of going away to that islet and building a wooden hut there and burning a few years out rowing to and fro fishing, or lying on the island slopes by day, and listening at night to the ripple of the water and the quivering of the bushes — full always of unknown creatures — and going out at morning to see the island's edge marked by the feet of birds.

MEMORY HARBOUR *by Jack B. Yeats (1871–1957)*.

'*Memory Harbour is a village of Rosses Point, but with the distances shortened and the houses run together as in an old-fashioned panoramic map. The man on the pedestal in the middle of the river is 'the metal man', and he points to where the water is deep enough for ships. The coffin, cross-bones, skull, and loaf at the point of the headland are to remind one of the sailor who was buried there by a ship's crew in a hurry not to miss the tide. As they were not sure if he was really dead they buried with him a loaf as the story runs.*

W.B.Y.'

It must be of interest to remember that the idyllic lines about a lake-island in Sligo followed R. L. Stevenson, a doomed exile, to Samoa and that he, remembering moorlands where about the graves of the martyrs the whaups were crying, was much moved by the poem.

Yeats, as happens to most of us, was to grow up and make his own terms with London, perhaps, to begin with, through those companions of the Cheshire Cheese, whom we are to meet later in this book. He was to walk a reasonable path between the Shavian

14

aggression and the Wildean social success, ending in catastrophe. Richard Ellmann has pointed out in that most valuable book, *Yeats: The Man and the Masks*, that while in London, and at the age of twenty-two years, Yeats was painfully introspective:

… self-conscious and aware of the vast gulf between what he was in actuality and what he was in his dreams. Eleven years before, Bernard Shaw had made the same crossing of the Irish Sea, and had found similar difficulty in adapting himself. Shaw says, in his preface to his early novel, Immaturity, *that he was too shy to accept invitations, and therefore hid his timidity under arrogance much as Yeats did: 'Clever sympathetic women might divine at a glance that I was mortally shy; but people who could not see through my skin, and who were accustomed to respect, and even veneration, from the young, may well have found me insufferable, aggressive and impudent.' Yeats, without the powerful epigrams with which Shaw drove the English before him, and by nature far more introspective and dreamy, was even more conscious of his own clumsiness. He remembered all his life how Oscar Wilde disapproved of the colour of his shoes and [he] felt that he was constantly committing* gaffes …

But Dublin City, for obvious and multiple reasons, was a more complicated matter than what the poet saw of mighty London. Dublin was painfully close to the bone. It was, after all, the capital of Ireland, and those great shadows of the eighteenth century – Burke, Goldsmith, Grattan – still moved there or, transmuted into stone, stood high on pedestals and looked down on the 'casual comedy'. It was the chief city in Yeats' life and the one in which he was to suffer sorely from that 'barren passion'; it was where he was to become involved in the pregnancy pains of national resurgence, and to found a national theatre and a theatrical tradition against varieties of opposition ranging from religious colly-wobbles to bred-in-the bone ignorance or, if you care to be grand about it, philistinism.

To create a fuss about commemorating Theobald Wolfe Tone or about not honouring Queen Victoria's Jubilee might seem to many, nowadays, to be both sad and at the same time comic. It was by no means so in the 1890s. It was the genuine wish of the poet to be counted one with Davis, Mangan and Ferguson; as genuine as his confidence, later, that he would take his place, at journey's end, with Landor and with Donne.

Matters came to the peak or the pit, no pun

intended, with the riot in the theatre over the production of *The Playboy of the Western World*. The scene at the public debate that followed the riot has been described by Mary Colum in her book *Life and the Dream*. At the time of the debate she was one of a group of young college-women, worshippers of Yeats. She was afterwards to marry the poet Padraic Colum, whose friendship I was honoured to have in his late years and at whose graveside I was privileged to speak. That was above Red Rock, high on Howth Head, in what Brendan Behan, in the genial way he had, described as the healthiest cemetery in Ireland.

But about that riot and/or debate, Mary Colum wrote:

A motley mixture of workmen, students, and bourgeoisie in evening dress filled the theatre, most of them with denunciatory speeches ready to deliver. Yeats took the platform in full evening dress and faced the crowd. Step by step he interpreted the play, delivering in the process some of his most complex theories of art, one moment cowing the audience, the next shouted down by them …

Even on the patriotics Yeats was equal to them, 'The author of Cathleen Ni Houlihan *addresses you,' he said.*

The audience, remembering that passionately patriotic play, forgot its antagonism for a few moments and Yeats got his cheers. At one moment a student supporter of his took the platform beside Yeats and made a remark which caused nearly all of the few women in the audience to walk out.

Myself and another girl student were the only members of the female sex in sight. We were surrounded by a group of angry males, ordering us, if we were virtuous girls, to leave the theatre. We stood our ground, and Yeats who, in spite of his well-publicized dimness of vision, could always see when it suited him, saw our difficulties from the platform and sent a couple of theatre attendants to escort us to the stalls among the men in evening dress, who, however, did not regard us with a friendly eye either.

I never witnessed a human being fight as Yeats fought that night, nor knew another with so meany weapons in his armoury.

It was, as another Irish poet said about something else altogether, so unimaginably different and all so long ago. But if Dublin is now the distinguished city of theatre that it is, then we owe that to William Yeats, and the impulse and inspiration have passed on to every part of the country.

Yeats' career, his trials and his triumph were most admirably sketched by Norman Jeffares in a talk delivered on Radio Eireann, as one of the Thomas Davis lectures set up by the novelist Francis MacManus and the poet Robert Farren. That particular set of talks was spear-headed and edited by Denis Donoghue, and also contained valuable talks by T. R. Henn, Frank Kermode and Donald Davie, later to be published by R. E. and the Mercier Press under the apt title *The Integrity of Yeats*. Jeffares said:

Before his marriage in 1917, Yeats had indeed experienced two extremes of public life: a youthful creative period filled with the illusion that his cultural movement would remodel an ideal idiosyncratic state on heroic models deriving from earlier Gaelic literature, a period filled by, as he said, creation without toil. Then had come the period of toil when creation seemed unwelcomed by the public he had hoped to bring into being. This was a period of disillusion, even of negativity. Yeats became a public figure of a different kind: from a youthful, idealistic revolutionary he merged into a middle-aged fighter for others' work. As the literary movement gained strength and reputation, so the forces of philistinism created greater obstacles. Ireland, the druid land he had celebrated in delicate druid tones, now became a blind bitter land in the astringency of his middle period. He had hauled others up the craggy heights of patriotic fervour when Cathleen Ni Houlihan *was performed; when Synge and Lane seemed likely to be thrown down where Parnell's memory lay, he had himself descended the declivities, in order to assert the rightful place of his friends upon the peaks of public life.*

By the time of his marriage, then, Yeats had experienced the heights and depths of public life, just as his work had swung from a romantic extreme to a realistic extreme. Now suddenly, almost miraculously, came the great flowering: now he began the new exciting poetry, founded in part upon the thoughts of his book, A Vision, *with all its vast view of history, of man, and of the supernatural; in part upon his own life. His poetry could now include both beauty and realism: magically he fused these extremes into poetry of emotive rhetoric. He could use both self and soul in the one poem and compel them into a unity of poetic personality. He symbolized his part in Irish life by living in a Norman tower in Galway; he had a daughter and son and so the old Yeats line would continue; the Nobel Prize for poetry was awarded to the poet Dublin had wrongly imagined 'finished'; the Abbey Theatre had become part of Dublin's life; and he, the erstwhile revolutionary, became a Senator of the Irish Free State.*

What is offered here is a brief and simple introduction to a great poet and to something of his background in the country from which he came. He lived and moved, in body and spirit, in more places than Ireland. But since he began there we may also dare to begin at the beginning. Yet this glimpse of his Ireland can be but a suggestion of, or a twitching of the curtain on, his vision of the world we endure in, or the worlds beyond, which most of us may never, nor ever wish to, attain. In the text that follows, my own words precede those of the poet and introduce each of his collections, as well as extracts from his prose.

As for the commentators and/or critics: some works are mentioned in the course of this text. Begin with them. They are all valuable. And the work of Norman Jeffares is now readily available. His original biography appeared ten years after the poet's death, but a new extended and amplified version has recently appeared (Hutchinson, 1988). And when you have read all that, go on from there. John Unterecker provides a bibliography that would daunt Marco Polo. The learned academics, in spite of or, perhaps, because of what he said about them, cannot fail to be of interest. But, better still, go back to all of the poetry and work it out for yourself.

The plays are another matter, another world. Because of the mission that Yeats felt upon him he needed, and he created, a theatre. But the plays, from *The Countess Cathleen* to *The Death of Cuchulain*, are all and essentially part of that same unity with which the poet hammered his thoughts. As a Vergilian guide through that world I cannot do better than recommend John Rees Moore in his *Masks of Love and Death: Yeats as Dramatist* (Cornell University Press, 1971).

Those of us who are troubled by political matters of the early 1930s may consult Richard Ellmann and Conor Cruise O'Brien: not separately but together. And we should avoid trying to be wise with hindsight, a risky form of acrobatics.

For a general background to the period I refer you to that most devoted of Yeatsians, Ulick O'Connor, in his *The Celtic Dawn* (Hamish Hamilton, 1984). And there is, always and for ever, George Moore.

POETRY

The stars are threshed, and the souls are threshed from their husks.   WILLIAM BLAKE

TO A.E.

The making of choices and the resultant exclusion of any, and much loved, poems is a painful process. Nor, in the long run, is there any substitute for the slow and careful consideration of the complete works. But that will come, must come. Let us begin here, stepping carefully. The poet himself, as we have mentioned, thought that, as the years went by, one poem would light up another and, through the poems, his myths and images would explain themselves.

The dedication to this collection, made when the poet was twenty-four years of age, is of significance, as is the epigraph from William Blake: a poet and prophet and artist who then, and for ever afterwards, was of supreme importance to William Yeats. In one of the great projects of his youth Yeats 'engaged upon the study of the Prophetic Books [of Blake] with "a view of producing a comprehensive edition of Blake's mystical writings, with all the original illustrations to the books and an elaborate commentary." ' His fellow-editor was his father's friend, Edwin J. Ellis, painter and poet. That work, undertaken in the devotion of youth, and for a material reward that now seems laughable, was to leave an impression on his mind and on his writing. Yeats' father had encouraged him in his enthusiasm for Blake but was more reserved, to say the least, about the beginnings of his friendship with George Russell who, for mystical reasons, adopted the pseudonym of A.E. John Yeats said of Russell that he was 'a saint but reared in Portadown', thereby paying tribute to the man's ethical and spiritual standing, which were to endure and magnify with the passing of the years, and also being gently humorous about a decent, but dull, Ulster town. He also observed that Russell had no love for, no admiration for, the individual man: 'He is too religious to care for really mortal things, or rather, for he does care, to admire and love them.'

With hindsight, and with our full knowledge of Russell (forget the absurd pseudonym) as he moved on from the intensity of youth through his middle years, which he made most helpful to other and younger writers, that judgment by John Yeats seems harsh. The novelist, George Moore, talked of the maieutic A. E. Mockery came easily to Moore, yet there was a real seriousness and a genuine tribute in his remark. And even though W. B. Yeats was later, for a while, to think that some of the young poets whom Russell encouraged had become facile imitators of Yeats himself, and to ask, rather nastily, if there was ever a dog that loved its fleas, and even though the best of friendships are liable to occasional strains, his respect for Russell was seldom to be questioned.

John B. Yeats, though, could at that particular time have been casting the eye of a nineteenth-century rationalist on just those highways of the spirit that the two young men were treading together: on the Dublin Hermetic Society, on Baron Reichenbach and Odic Force, on Madame Blavatsky and on the Dublin Theosophical Lodge, and even on Babu Mohini Chaterjee, a Brahmin from Bengal who brightened (he must certainly have done so) Dublin by a visit. About this remarkable man, William Yeats in later years wrote:

He taught us by what seemed an invincible logic that those who die, in so far as they have imagined beauty or justice, are made part of that beauty or justice and move through the minds of living men, as Shelley believed; and that mind overshadows mind, even among the living, and by pathways that lie beyond the senses; and that he measured labour by this measure and put the hermit above all other labourers, because being the most silent and the most hidden, he lived nearer to the Eternal Powers, and showed their mastery of the world. Alcibiades fled from Socrates lest he might do nothing but listen to him all life long, and I am certain that we, seeking, as youth will, for some unknown deed or thought, all dreamed that but to listen to this man, who threw the enchantment of powers about silent and gentle things, and at last to think as he did, was the one thing worth doing and thinking, and that action and all words that lead to action were a little vulgar, a little trivial. Ah, how many years it has taken me to wake out of that dream.

Crossways, indeed! And the Indian influences are evident in this 1889 collection, most notably in the poems 'Anashuya and Vijaya' and 'The Indian Upon God'.

But for our present purposes we will travel mostly on the little roads of Ireland, with the beauty of the Sligo countryside, and glenside and lakeside, as reflected in the poem about the human child taken by the Good People (p. 20); and with the salley gardens and one of the loveliest love-songs of our time (p. 21); and with the old fisherman on the Sligo shore (p. 24) meditating on time and better catches of salmon, and on more beautiful young women than the present had to offer to his aged eyes; and with such authentic country people of the Ireland of the poet's youth as Father O'Hart (p. 22); and with the tale of the dying huntsman (p. 25), which owed something to the early nineteenth-century novelist, Gerald Griffin, of *The Collegians* and *Tales of the Munster Festivals* and much more.

Where dips the rocky highland
Of Sleuth Wood in the lake,
There lies a leafy island
Where flapping herons wake
The drowsy water-rats;
There we've hid our faery vats,
Full of berries
And of reddest stolen cherries.
Come away, O human child!
To the waters and the wild
With a faery, hand in hand,
For the world's more full of weeping
than you can understand.

Where the wave of moonlight glosses
The dim grey sands with light,
Far off by furthest Rosses
We foot it all the night,
Weaving olden dances,
Mingling hands and mingling glances
Till the moon has taken flight;
To and fro we leap
And chase the frothy bubbles,
While the world is full of troubles
And is anxious in its sleep.
Come away, O human child!
To the waters and the wild
With a faery, hand in hand,
For the world's more full of weeping
than you can understand.

Where the wandering water gushes
From the hills above Glen-Car,
In pools among the rushes
That scarce could bathe a star,
We seek for slumbering trout
And whispering in their ears
Give them unquiet dreams;
Leaning softly out
From ferns that drop their tears
Over the young streams.
Come away, O human child!
To the waters and the wild
With a faery, hand in hand,
For the world's more full of weeping
than you can understand.

Away with us he's going,
The solemn-eyed:
He'll hear no more the lowing
Of the calves on the warm hillside
Or the kettle on the hob
Sing peace into his breast,
Or see the brown mice bob
Round and round the oatmeal-chest.
For he comes, the human child,
To the waters and the wild
With a faery, hand in hand,
From a world more full of weeping
than he can understand.

DOWN BY THE SALLEY GARDENS

Down by the salley gardens my love and I did meet;
She passed the salley gardens with little snow-white feet.
She bid me take love easy, as the leaves grow on the tree;
But I, being young and foolish, with her would not agree.

In a field by the river my love and I did stand,
And on my leaning shoulder she laid her snow-white hand.
She bid me take life easy, as the grass grows on the weirs;
But I was young and foolish, and now am full of tears.

Glencar Falls, County Sligo.
Turn into the mountains from Drumcliff and
you will find yourself at the magic waterfall.

Good Father John O'Hart
In penal days rode out
To a shoneen who had free lands
And his own snipe and trout.

In trust took he John's lands;
Sleiveens were all his race;
And he gave them as dowers to his daughters,
And they married beyond their place.

But Father John went up,
And Father John went down;
And he wore small holes in his shoes,
And he wore large holes in his gown.

All loved him, only the shoneen,
Whom the devils have by the hair,
From the wives, and the cats, and the children,
To the birds in the white of the air.

The birds, for he opened their cages
As he went up and down;
And he said with a smile, 'Have peace now';
And he went his way with a frown.

But if when anyone died
Came keeners hoarser than rooks,
He bade them give over their keening;
For he was a man of books.

And these were the works of John,
When, weeping score by score,
People came into Colooney;
For he'd died at ninety-four.

There was no human keening;
The birds from Knocknarea
And the world round Knocknashee
Came keening in that day.

The young birds and old birds
Came flying, heavy and sad;
Keening in from Tiraragh,
Keening from Ballinafad;

Keening from Inishmurray,
Nor stayed for bite or sup;
This way were all reproved
Who dig old customs up.

A Connacht priest of the time, as Jack B. Yeats saw him.

23

THE MEDITATION OF THE OLD FISHERMAN

You waves, though you dance by my feet like children at play,
Though you glow and you glance, though you purr and you dart;
In the Junes that were warmer than these are, the waves were more gay,
When I was a boy with never a crack in my heart.

The herring are not in the tides as they were of old;
My sorrow! for many a creak gave the creel in the cart
That carried the take to Sligo town to be sold,
When I was a boy with never a crack in my heart.

And ah, you proud maiden, you are not so fair when his oar
Is heard on the water, as they were, the proud and apart,
Who paced in the eve by the nets on the pebbly shore,
When I was a boy with never a crack in my heart.

GLENCAR SLIGO. 5032 W.L.

'Lay me in a cushioned chair;
Carry me, ye four,
With cushions here and cushions there,
To see the world once more.

'To stable and to kennel go;
Bring what is there to bring;
Lead my Lollard to and fro,
Or gently in a ring.

'Put the chair upon the grass:
Bring Rody and his hounds,
That I may contented pass
From these earthly bounds.'

His eyelids droop, his head falls low,
His old eyes cloud with dreams;
The sun upon all things that grow
Falls in sleepy streams.

Brown Lollard treads upon the lawn,
And to the armchair goes,
And now the old man's dreams are gone,
He smooths the long brown nose.

And now moves many a pleasant tongue
Upon his wasted hands,
For leading aged hounds and young
The huntsman near him stands.

'Huntsman Rody, blow the horn,
Make the hills reply.'
The huntsman loosens on the morn
A gay wandering cry.

Fire is in the old man's eyes,
His fingers move and sway,
And when the wandering music dies
They hear him feebly say,

'Huntsman Rody, blow the horn,
Make the hills reply.'
'I cannot blow upon my horn,
I can but weep and sigh.'

Servants round his cushioned place
Are with new sorrow wrung;
Hounds are gazing on his face,
Aged hounds and young.

One blind hound only lies apart
On the sun-smitten grass;
He holds deep commune with his heart:
The moments pass and pass;

The blind hound with a mournful din
Lifts slow his wintry head;
The servants bear the body in;
The hounds wail for the dead.

THE OLD HUNTSMAN

Sero te amavi, Pulchritudo tam antiqua et tam nova!
Sero te amavi.   ST AUGUSTINE

TO LIONEL JOHNSON

One may suppose that any, or every, young poet should be entitled to borrow an epigraph from Saint Augustine. That good African member of the Roman Empire had his problems, which he may have solved to his own satisfaction but never quite to mine. Young poets belong in his curious country.

The poet to whom this collection was dedicated would, though, because of his religion and because of a certain morbidity of temperament, have meditated much on Augustine. Of Lionel Johnson, one of the 'tragic generation', one of the poets with whom, Yeats said, he learned his trade, one of the Rhymers' Club – his 'companions of the Cheshire Cheese' in Fleet Street, London – Yeats later wrote in *The Trembling of the Veil* that there was not any branch of knowledge that Johnson, who had his Irish connections and loyalties, did not claim for his own. A strange and lonely man, who wrote that great poem on the statue of King Charles at Charing Cross and who died sadly.

The man who thought so imaginatively, and thought so highly of the profession of man of letters, must have been moved to read the dedication to a collection of poems that invokes the Rose, everlasting symbol of beauty (p. 31), a collection that looks back to the deep-woven shadows of ancient Ireland and the heroic legend of Cuchulain (p. 28) – the greatest of all heroes, the sunlike image of the brave and noble man the young poet may have wished to become. Cuchulain and his legend, noble and tragic, are to stay with the poet to the end.

There are two versions of how the first meeting took place between William Yeats and Maud Gonne, the beautiful and inspirational revolutionary, 'the trouble of my life'. She was later to write that she met Yeats in Dublin at the residence of John O'Leary, the noble old survivor of the Fenian Rising of 1867, where she heard Yeats read poetry, and afterwards he walked her home and carried her books. He remembered her first appearing at Bedford Park in London, bearing a letter from John O'Leary to his father, John B. Yeats. Men and women being as they are, both versions are probably true.

She was to be his torment and inspiration for many years and she and O'Leary were to draw him somewhat, and in his own way, into Irish revolutionary causes. But above all she was to draw from him some of his noblest poetry, as in the famous lines of 'When You Are Old' (p. 32), which open with a distant echo of Ronsard.

Like the poet, Maud Gonne was familiar with the Hill of Howth, or Howth Head, which is, you might say, the strong left arm that guards the north of Dublin Bay. It has its associations with Celtic mythology and also with English Elizabethan poetry, in that Edmund Spenser, of *The Faerie Queene*, made landfall in the neighbourhood when he first came to Ireland.

For a while in Yeats' youth his father, painter and man of humour and wisdom, found a residence, or two residences one after the other, in or on Howth, and the lonely places on the great hill or head meant much to the young man, who was night-walker, and naturalist, and seeker after solitude.

Later in life, and after he had encountered Maud Gonne, it gave the place a special importance to know that she had lived there as a child and had loved its beauty and its solitude. She wrote about it:

No place has ever seemed to me quite so lovely as Howth was then ... The heather grew so high and strong there that we could make cubby houses and be entirely hidden and entirely warm and sheltered from the strong wind ... After I was grown up I have often slept all night in that friendly

heather ... From deep down in it one looks up at the stars in a wonderful security and falls asleep to wake up only with the call of the sea birds looking for their breakfast.

Yeats remembered a day that he had spent with Maud Gonne on the cliffs of Howth, looking down on the bay and the Bailey lighthouse, and in memory of that day came the poem first published in 1890, 'The White Birds' (p. 34).

His 'Dedication to a Book of Stories selected from the Irish Novelists' of the early part of the century (p. 37) displayed his affection, and critical respect, for William Carleton, Charles Lever, Samuel Lover and others, for the tales they had to tell and the background from which they drew. His old pensioner spitting in the face of transience and Time (p. 37) could easily have been at home in Ned McKeown's house at Kilrudden crossroads in the Clogher Valley of South Tyrone, in Carleton's *Traits and Stories of the Irish Peasantry*.

And in the final poem in the selection, 'To Ireland in the Coming Times' (p. 39) the poet claims his place with Thomas Davis, enlightened patriot of the 1840s and writer of patriotic verse, with James Clarence Mangan, a greater poet by far than Davis, who had also caught echoes from the Gaelic past, and with Samuel Ferguson, a scholar whose poetry could reach up to and find epical quality. But in that poem Yeats also states his attachment, or addiction, to the shadowy ways into which his thoughts on Celtic Druidism, and on William Blake, and on hermetic and magical matters had led him.

He was creating or discovering, and following his symbols, and also, we must never forget, searching for truth.

A man came slowly from the setting sun,
To Emer, raddling raiment in her dun,
And said, 'I am that swineherd whom you bid
Go watch the road between the wood and tide,
But now I have no need to watch it more.'

Then Emer cast the web upon the floor,
And raising arms all raddled with the dye,
Parted her lips with a loud sudden cry.

That swinehead stared upon her face and said,
'No man alive, no man among the dead,
Has won the gold his cars of battle bring.'

'But if your master comes home triumphing
Why must you blench and shake from foot to crown?'

Thereon he shook the more and cast him down
Upon the web-heaped floor, and cried his word:
'With him is one sweet-throated like a bird.'

'You dare me to my face,' and thereupon
She smote with raddled fist, and where her son
Herded the cattle came with stumbling feet,
And cried with angry voice, 'It is not meet
To idle life away, a common herd.'

'I have long waited, mother, for that word:
But wherefore now?'
                        'There is a man to die;
You have the heaviest arm under the sky.'

'Whether under its daylight or its stars
My father stands amid his battle-cars.'

'But you have grown to be the taller man.'

'Yet somewhere under starlight or the sun
My father stands.'
                    'Aged, worn out with wars
On foot, on horseback or in battle-cars.'

'I only ask what way my journey lies,
For He who made you bitter made you wise.'

'The Red Branch camp in a great company
Between wood's rim and the horses of the sea.
Go there, and light a camp-fire at wood's rim;
But tell your name and lineage to him
Whose blade compels, and wait till they have found
Some feasting man that the same oath has bound.'

Among those feasting men Cuchulain dwelt,
And his young sweetheart close beside him knelt,
Stared on the mournful wonder of his eyes,
Even as Spring upon the ancient skies,
And pondered on the glory of his days;
And all around the harp-string told his praise,
And Conchubar, the Red Branch king of kings,
With his own fingers touched the brazen strings.

At last Cuchulain spake, 'Some man has made
His evening fire amid the leafy shade.
I have often heard him singing to and fro,
I have often heard the sweet sound of his bow.
Seek out what man he is.'
                            One went and came.
'He bade me let all know he gives his name
At the sword-point, and waits till we have found
Some feasting man that the same oath has bound.'

Cuchulain cried, 'I am the only man
Of all this host so bound from childhood on.'

After short fighting in the leafy shade,
He spake to the young man, 'Is there no maid
Who loves you, no white arms to wrap you round,
Or do you long for the dim sleepy ground,
That you have come and dared me to my face?'

'The dooms of men are in God's hidden place.'

'Your head a while seemed like a woman's head
That I loved once.'
                        Again the fighting sped,
But now the war-rage in Cuchulain woke,
And through that new blade's guard the old blade
    broke,
And pierced him.
                        'Speak before your breath is done.'

'Cuchulain I, mighty Cuchulain's son.'

'I put you from your pain. I can no more.'

While day its burden on to evening bore,
With head bowed on his knees Cuchulain stayed;
Then Conchubar sent that sweet-throated maid,
And she, to win him, his grey hair caressed;
In vain her arms, in vain her soft white breast.
Then Conchubar, the subtlest of all men,
Ranking his Druids round him ten by ten,
Spake thus: 'Cuchulain will dwell there and brood
For three days more in dreadful quietude,
And then arise, and raving slay us all.
Chaunt in his ear delusions magical,
That he may fight the horses of the sea.'
The Druids took them to their mystery,
And chaunted for three days.
                              Cuchulain stirred,
Stared on the horses of the sea, and heard
The cars of battle and his own name cried;
And fought with the invulnerable tide.

William Carleton. 'The greatest novelist of Ireland
by right of the most Celtic eyes that ever gazed
from under the brow of a storyteller.'
   Letters to the New Island, 1934, W.B. Yeats

THE LAKE ISLE OF INNISFREE

I will arise and go now, and go to Innisfree,
And a small cabin build there, of clay and wattles made:
Nine bean-rows will I have there, a hive for the honey-bee,
And live alone in the bee-loud glade.

And I shall have some peace there, for peace comes dropping slow,
Dropping from the veils of the morning to where the cricket sings;
There midnight's all a glimmer, and noon a purple glow,
And evening full of the linnet's wings.

I will arise and go now, for always night and day
I hear lake water lapping with low sounds by the shore;
While I stand on the roadway, or on the pavements grey,
I hear it in the deep heart's core.

THE ROSE OF THE WORLD

Who dreamed that beauty passes like a dream?
For these red lips, with all their mournful pride,
Mournful that no new wonder may betide,
Troy passed away in one high funeral gleam,
And Usna's children died.

We and the labouring world are passing by:
Amid men's souls, that waver and give place
Like the pale waters in their wintry race,
Under the passing stars, foam of the sky,
Lives on this lonely face.

Bow down, archangels, in your dim abode:
Before you were, or any hearts to beat,
Weary and kind one lingered by His seat;
He made the world to be a grassy road
Before her wandering feet.

Lough Gill, County Sligo.

THE PITY OF LOVE

A pity beyond all telling
Is hid in the heart of love:
The folk who are buying and selling,
The clouds on their journey above,
The cold wet winds ever blowing,
And the shadowy hazel grove
Where mouse-grey waters are flowing,
Threaten the head that I love.

THE SORROW OF LOVE

The brawling of a sparrow in the eaves,
The brilliant moon and all the milky sky,
And all that famous harmony of leaves,
Had blotted out man's image and his cry.

A girl arose that had red mournful lips
And seemed the greatness of the world in tears,
Doomed like Odysseus and the labouring ships
And proud as Priam murdered with his peers;

Arose, and on the instant clamorous eaves,
A climbing moon upon an empty sky,
And all that lamentation of the leaves,
Could but compose man's image and his cry.

WHEN YOU ARE OLD

When you are old and grey and full of sleep,
And nodding by the fire, take down this book,
And slowly read, and dream of the soft look
Your eyes had once, and of their shadows deep;

How many loved your moments of glad grace,
And loved your beauty with love false or true,
But one man loved the pilgrim soul in you,
And loved the sorrows of your changing face;

And bending down beside the glowing bars,
Murmur, a little sadly, how Love fled
And paced upon the mountains overhead
And hid his face amid a crowd of stars.

Maud Gonne.

*'And that proud look as though she had gazed into
the burning sun,
And all the shapely body no tittle gone astray.'*
'His Phoenix'

32

THE WHITE BIRDS

I would that we were, my beloved, white birds on the foam of the sea!
We tire of the flame of the meteor, before it can fade and flee;
And the flame of the blue star of twilight, hung low on the rim of the sky,
Has awaked in our hearts, my beloved, a sadness that may not die.

A weariness comes from those dreamers, dew-dabbled, the lily and rose;
Ah, dream not of them, my beloved, the flame of the meteor that goes,
Or the flame of the blue star that lingers hung low in the fall of the dew:
For I would we were changed to white birds on the wandering foam: I and you!

I am haunted by numberless islands, and many a Danaan shore,
Where Time would surely forget us, and Sorrow come near us no more;
Soon far from the rose and the lily and fret of the flames would we be,
Were we only white birds, my beloved, buoyed out on the foam of the sea!

A BREEZY DAY, HOWTH, *c.1910,*
by William Orpen (1878–1931).

LOOKING AT THE SEA, HOWTH,
c.1910 by William Orpen.

'Oh storyteller, do not tire
Between the fire and the wall ...'
The poet Austin Clarke (1893–1974).

THE LAMENTATION OF THE OLD PENSIONER

Although I shelter from the rain
Under a broken tree,
My chair was nearest to the fire
In every company
That talked of love or politics,
Ere Time transfigured me.

Though lads are making pikes again
For some conspiracy,
And crazy rascals rage their fill
At human tyranny,
My contemplations are of Time
That has transfigured me.

There's not a woman turns her face
Upon a broken tree,
And yet the beauties that I loved
Are in my memory;
I spit into the face of Time
That has transfigured me.

THE DEDICATION TO A BOOK OF STORIES
SELECTED FROM THE IRISH NOVELISTS

There was a green branch hung with many a bell
When her own people ruled this tragic Eire;
And from its murmuring greenness, calm of Faery,
A Druid kindness, on all hearers fell.

It charmed away the merchant from his guile,
And turned the farmer's memory from his cattle,
And hushed in sleep the roaring ranks of battle:
And all grew friendly for a little while.

Ah, Exiles wandering over lands and seas,
And planning, plotting always that some morrow
May set a stone upon ancestral Sorrow!
I also bear a bell-branch full of ease.

I tore it from green boughs winds tore and tossed
Until the sap of summer had grown weary!
I rode it from the barren boughs of Eire,
That country where a man can be so crossed;

Can be so battered, badgered and destroyed
That he's a loveless man: gay bells bring laughter
That shakes a mouldering cobweb from the rafter;
And yet the saddest chimes are best enjoyed.

Gay bells or sad, they bring you memories
Of half-forgotten innocent old places:
We and our bitterness have left no traces
On Munster grass and Connemara skies.

'We and our bitterness have left no traces
On Munster grass and Connemara skies.'

EARLY MORNING IN CONNEMARA
by Maurice MacGonigal (1900–79).

Know, that I would accounted be
True brother of a company
That sang, to sweeten Ireland's wrong,
Ballad and story, rann and song;
Nor be I any less of them,
Because the red-rose-bordered hem
Of her, whose history began
Before God made the angelic clan,
Trails all about the written page.
When Time began to rant and rage
The measure of her flying feet
Made Ireland's heart begin to beat;
And Time bade all his candles flare
To light a measure here and there;
And may the thoughts of Ireland brood
Upon a measured quietude.

Nor may I less be counted one
With Davis, Mangan, Ferguson,
Because, to him who ponders well,
My rhymes more than their rhyming tell
Of things discovered in the deep,
Where only body's laid asleep.
For the elemental creatures go
About my table to and fro,
That hurry from unmeasured mind
To rant and rage in flood and wind;
Yet he who treads in measured ways
May surely barter gaze for gaze.
Man ever journeys on with them
After the red-rose-bordered hem.
Ah, faeries, dancing under the moon,
A Druid land, a Druid tune!

While still I may, I write for you
The love I lived, the dream I knew.
From our birthday, until we die,
Is but the winking of an eye;
And we, our singing and our love,
What measurer Time has lit above,
And all benighted things that go
About my table to and fro,
Are passing on to where may be,
In truth's consuming ecstasy,
No place for love and dream at all;
For God goes by with white footfall.
I cast my heart into my rhymes,
That you, in the dim coming times,
May know how my heart went with them
After the red-rose-bordered hem.

The very title of this collection links it with lonely landscapes and chaste, bird-haunted lakes in the western parts of this island. But Yeats, at the time of its appearance, had many other matters to the fore in a crowded mind. He had lived in London and walked there and had, as we have seen, remembered Lough Gill and the island that became known to the world as Innisfree. He had moved in London, as of right, in the artistic circles frequented by his father and had been for ever impressed by the social theories and the writings of William Morris, in verse and prose, particularly in, say, such a measured romance as *The Sundering Flood.*

The century was coming to an end. He was approaching the mid-point of his life. He had become involved in several ways in 'The seeming needs of [his] fool-driven land', in Irish literary groups in London and in Dublin, in matters political, even becoming for a while a member of the secret (although how secret one may, in Ireland, be permitted to wonder) revolutionary organization, the Irish Republican Brotherhood. What he was later to describe, if not to lament, as a 'barren passion' had set his mind in a tumult and strengthened, if not actually created, his links, such as they were, with those revolutionary ideas.

There had been, in 1897, Irish protests against any celebration in Dublin of the Jubilee of that other *femme fatale*, Queen Victoria, and, in 1898, the nationalist commemoration of the fatal year of rebellion of 1798 and of the name of Theobald Wolfe Tone, the tragic figure whom we still describe as the Father of the Irish Republic.

About all Yeats had become involved, as the central figure, with some dear friends, already mentioned – and with others neither so dear nor so friendly – in the creation of an Irish theatre, the greatest gift, after his poetry, that he gave to his country. His first two plays, *The Countess Cathleen* and *The Land of Heart's Desire*, had appeared.

About the collection *The Wind Among the Reeds* Joseph Hone wrote:

In picturesque apposition to his politics were Yeats' new lyrics, The Wind Among the Reeds, *and his new dramatic poem, 'The Shadowy Waters'. On its publication, in 1899,* The Wind Among the Reeds *was highly praised by Arthur Symons, and by a few critics, and this book still represents to some older readers, hardly to any of the young, the high-water-mark of Yeats' lyricism. That he had advanced in technical accomplishment admitted of no doubt. There was far less of unnecessary beauty than in the earlier volume; he was no longer carried away by every fancy into the side images which marred the directness of the 'Rose' poems. The more characteristic, the dimmer and more esoteric poems in* The Wind Among the Reeds, *those which bear the signature of what he afterwards called a dream-burdened will, create a curious effect of isolation in the whole body of the work; and it is significant that of all his books this was the one that he revised least for republication. These lyrics must be pre-Raphaelite or nothing.*

The Rose that blossomed in the deeps of his heart could be pre-Raphaelite, but the story of O'Driscoll (p. 44), whose wife was taken by the Good People, could have a connection with the tragic case of Brigid Cleary, some of whose people thought she had been so taken, at Ballyvadlea near Clonmel in County Tipperary, in 1895. A sad story, and one that would give any man reason to brood, in sombre fashion, upon ancient quietude. Reality is always a shock.

Here too, in this collection, the poet takes the image of Wandering Aengus (p. 44) from the assembly of Celtic deities and follows him in his endless quest for love and beauty – endless, and with little hope except in the quest itself.

It pleases and amuses me to remember that one morning, in the Burren of County Clare, I met an American poet who asked me to lead him to a hazel wood, where he went through the appropriate ritual; then to lead him to the lake at Corofin and to set him out in a boat a-fishing. He had never fished, nor tried to, in his life before that day, but he solemnly assured me that he wanted to get the feel of the business.

When all else is dumb, as the man said, poetry cries out aloud.

Finally to 'The Fiddler of Dooney' (p. 46): I know that I must have seen that man long ago at the horse-races on the sands of Mullaghmore on the Sligo coast.

Out-worn heart, in a time out-worn,
Come clear of the nets of wrong and right;
Laugh, heart, again in the grey twilight,
Sigh, heart, again in the dew of the morn.

Your mother Eire is always young,
Dew ever shining and twilight grey;
Though hope fall from you and love decay,
Burning in fires of a slanderous tongue.

Come, heart, where hill is heaped upon hill:
For there the mystical brotherhood
Of sun and moon and hollow and wood
And river and stream work out their will;

And God stands winding His lonely horn,
And time and the world are ever in flight;
And love is less kind than the grey twilight
And hope is less dear than the dew of the morn.

O'Driscoll drove with a song
The wild duck and the drake
From the tall and tufted reeds
Of the drear Hart Lake.

And he saw how the reeds grew dark
At the coming of night-tide,
And dreamed of the long dim hair
Of Bridget his bride.

He heard while he sang and dreamed
A piper piping away,
And never was piping so sad,
And never was piping so gay.

And he saw young men and young girls
Who danced on a level place,
And Bridget his bride among them,
With a sad and a gay face.

The dancers crowded about him
And many a sweet thing said,
And a young man brought him red wine
And a young girl white bread.

But Bridget drew him by the sleeve
Away from the merry bands,
To old men playing at cards
With a twinkling of ancient hands.

The bread and the wine had a doom,
For these were the host of the air;
He sat and played in a dream
Of her long dim hair.

He played with the merry old men
And thought not of evil chance,
Until one bore Bridget his bride
Away from the merry dance.

He bore her away in his arms,
The handsomest young man there,
And his neck and his breast and his arms
Were drowned in her long dim hair.

O'Driscoll scattered the cards
And out of his dream awoke:
Old men and young men and young girls
Were gone like a drifting smoke;

But he heard high up in the air
A piper piping away,
And never was piping so sad,
And never was piping so gay.

I went out to the hazel wood,
Because a fire was in my head,
And cut and peeled a hazel wand,
And hooked a berry to a thread;
And when white moths were on the wing,
And moth-like stars were flickering out,
I dropped the berry in a stream
And caught a little silver trout.

When I had laid it on the floor
I went to blow the fire aflame,
But something rustled on the floor,
And some one called me by my name,
It had become a glimmering girl
With apple blossom in her hair
Who called me by my name and ran
And faded through the brightening air.

Though I am old with wandering
Through hollow lands and hilly lands,
I will find out where she has gone,
And kiss her lips and take her hands;
And walk among long dappled grass,
And pluck till time and times are done
The silver apples of the moon,
The golden apples of the sun.

THE SECRET ROSE

Far-off, most secret, and inviolate Rose,
Enfold me in my hour of hours; where those
Who sought thee in the Holy Sepulchre,
Or in the wine-vat, dwell beyond the stir
And tumult of defeated dreams; and deep
Among pale eyelids, heavy with the sleep
Men have named beauty. Thy great leaves enfold
The ancient beards, the helms of ruby and gold
Of the crowned Magi; and the king whose eyes
Saw the Pierced Hands and Rood of elder rise
In Druid vapour and make the torches dim;
Till vain frenzy awoke and he died; and him
Who met Fand walking among flaming dew
By a grey shore where the wind never blew,
And lost the world and Emer for a kiss;
And him who drove the gods out of their liss,
And till a hundred morns had flowered red
Feasted, and wept the barrows of his dead;
And the proud dreaming king who flung the crown
And sorrow away, and calling bard and clown
Dwelt among wine-stained wanderers in deep woods;
And him who sold tillage, and house, and goods,

And sought through lands and islands numberless years,
Until he found, with laughter and with tears,
A woman of so shining loveliness
That men threshed corn at midnight by a tress,
A little stolen tress. I, too, await
The hour of thy great wind of love and hate.
When shall the stars be blown about the sky,
Like the sparks blown out of a smithy, and die?
Surely thine hour has come, thy great wind blows,
Far-off, most secret, and inviolate Rose?

THE SONG OF THE OLD MOTHER

I rise in the dawn, and I kneel and blow
Till the seed of the fire flicker and glow;
And then I must scrub and bake and sweep
Till stars are beginning to blink and peep;
And the young lie long and dream in their bed
Of the matching of ribbons for bosom and head,
And their day goes over in idleness,
And they sigh if the wind but lift a tress:
While I must work because I am old,
And the seed of the fire gets feeble and cold.

HE WISHES FOR THE CLOTHS OF HEAVEN

Had I the heavens' embroidered cloths,
Enwrought with golden and silver light,
The blue and the dim and the dark cloths
Of night and light and the half-light,
I would spread the cloths under your feet:
But I, being poor, have only my dreams;
I have spread my dreams under your feet;
Tread softly because you tread on my dreams.

THE LOVER SPEAKS TO THE HEARERS OF HIS SONGS
IN COMING DAYS

O women, kneeling by your altar-rails long hence,
When songs I wove for my beloved hide the prayer,
And smoke from this dead heart drifts through the violet air
And covers away the smoke of myrrh and frankincense;
Bend down and pray for all that sin I wove in song,
Till the Attorney for Lost Souls cry her sweet cry,
And call to my beloved and me: 'No longer fly
Amid the hovering, piteous, penitential throng.'

When I play on my fiddle in Dooney,
Folk dance like a wave of the sea;
My cousin is priest in Kilvarnet,
My brother in Mocharabuiee.*

I passed my brother and cousin:
They read in their books of prayer;
I read in my book of songs
I bought at the Sligo fair.

When we come at the end of time
To Peter sitting in state,
He will smile on the three old spirits,
But call me first through the gate;

For the good are always the merry,
Save by an evil chance,
And the merry love the fiddle,
And the merry love to dance:

And when the folk there spy me,
They will all come up to me,
With 'Here is the fiddler of Dooney!'
And dance like a wave of the sea.

*Pronounced as if spelt 'Mockrabwee'.

THE CROSSROADS DANCE IN
CONNACHT, *as it once upon a time was.*
A painting by Charles Lamb (1893–1964).

The momentous meeting that brought the poet to the Seven Woods and to the waters of Coole, close to the ancient town of Gort in County Galway, took place in 1898. Perhaps it is best to leave the account of that meeting to one of the two persons most involved: Augusta, Lady Gregory. This is how she wrote about it, in proper proprietorial fashion, in her book *Our Irish Theatre*.

Mr Edward Martyn came to seem me, bringing with him Mr Yeats whom I did not know very well, though I cared for his work very much and had already, through his directions, been gathering folklore. They had lunch with us, but it was a wet day and we could not go out ... We sat through the wet afternoon, and though I had never been at all interested in theatres, our talk turned on plays. Mr Martyn had written two, The Heather Field and Maeve. They had been offered to London managers, and now he thought of having them produced in Germany, where there seemed to be more room for new drama than in England. I said it was a pity we had no Irish theatre where such plays could be given. Mr Yeats said that had always been a dream of his, but he had of late thought it an impossible one, for it could not at first pay its way and there was no money to be found for such a thing in Ireland. We went on talking about it, and things seemed to grow possible as we talked, before the end of the afternoon we had made our plan. We said we would collect money, or rather ask to have a certain sum of money guaranteed. We would then take a Dublin theatre and give a performance of Mr Martyn's Heather Field, and one of Mr Yeats' own plays, The Countess Cathleen.

'Things seemed to grow possible as we talked ...' Now there was a reasonable, practical woman talking.

Gabriel Fallon, who was an Abbey Theatre actor away back and who, in his later years, was a sound critic of the theatre in Dublin, and much devoted to his memories of Lady Gregory, used frequently to quote that sentence to me as a general defence of the beneficial nature of reasonable discussion. He was strong on the practical mind of Augusta, Lady Gregory, and on how much it meant to Yeats, at that time in his life, to have that sanative refuge to withdraw to, in the woods of Coole. The poet himself, as we shall see, has spoken most memorably of that place, and that great house, and that great lady.

On the sea-coast at Duras, a few miles from Coole, an old French count, Florimond de Basterot, lived for certain months in every year. Lady Gregory and I talked over my project of an Irish Theatre, looking out upon the lawn of his house, watching a large flock of ducks that was always gathered for his arrival from Paris, and that would be a very small flock, if indeed it were a flock at all, when he set out for Rome in the autumn. I told her that I had given up my project because it was impossible to get the few pounds necessary for a start in little halls, and she promised to collect or give the money necessary. That was her first great service to the Irish intellectual movement.

Thus we find him 'In the Seven Woods' of Coole (p. 50) at the beginning of the century, brooding on agonized love, or following in the footsteps of the half-demented, red-headed poet Hanrahan (p. 51), perhaps an image of Red Owen O'Sullivan of the Sliabh tuachra poets; or seeing in vision 'The Happy Town-land' (p. 53) that poets, and even wise men, might wish to find and inhabit for ever.

AUGUSTA GREGORY, 1905,
by John Butler Yeats (1839–1922).

IN THE SEVEN WOODS

I have heard the pigeons of the Seven Woods
Make their faint thunder, and the garden bees
Hum in the lime-tree flowers; and put away
The unavailing outcries and the old bitterness
That empty the heart. I have forgot awhile
Tara uprooted, and new commonness
Upon the throne and crying about the streets
And hanging its paper flowers from post to post,
Because it is alone of all things happy.
I am contented, for I know that Quiet
Wanders laughing and eating her wild heart
Among pigeons and bees, while that Great Archer,
Who but awaits His hour to shoot, still hangs
A cloudy quiver over Pairc-na-lee.

August 1902

THE FOLLY OF BEING COMFORTED

One that is ever kind said yesterday:
'Your well-belovèd's hair has threads of grey,
And little shadows come about her eyes;
Time can but make it easier to be wise
Though now it seems impossible, and so
All that you need is patience.'

      Heart cries, 'No,
I have not a crumb of comfort, not a grain.
Time can but make her beauty over again:
Because of that great nobleness of hers
The fire that stirs about her, when she stirs,
Burns but more clearly. O she had not these ways
When all the wild summer was in her gaze.'

O heart! O heart! if she'd but turn her head,
You'd know the folly of being comforted.

COOLE PARK, COUNTY GALWAY
by W.B. Yeats.

The old brown thorn-trees break in two high over Cummen Strand,
Under a bitter black wind that blows from the left hand;
Our courage breaks like an old tree in a black wind and dies,
But we have hidden in our hearts the flame out of the eyes
Of Cathleen, the daughter of Houlihan.

The wind has bundled up the clouds high over Knocknarea,
And thrown the thunder on the stones for all that Maeve can say.
Angers that are like noisy clouds have set our hearts abeat;
But we have all bent low and low and kissed the quiet feet
Of Cathleen, the daughter of Houlihan.

The yellow pool has overflowed high up on Clooth-na-Bare,
For the wet winds are blowing out of the clinging air;
Like heavy flooded waters our bodies and our blood;
But purer than a tall candle before the Holy Rood
Is Cathleen, the daughter of Houlihan.

CATHLEEN NI HOULIHAN
by Sir John Lavery (1856–1941).

IRISH PIPER. 6620. W.L.

There's many a strong farmer
Whose heart would break in two,
If he could see the townland
That we are riding to;
Boughs have their fruit and blossom
At all times of the year;
Rivers are running over
With red beer and brown beer.
An old man plays the bagpipes
In a golden and silver wood;
Queens, their eyes blue like the ice,
Are dancing in a crowd.

The little fox he murmured,
'O what of the world's bane?'
The sun was laughing sweetly,
The moon plucked at my rein;
But the little red fox murmured,
'O do not pluck at his rein,
He is riding to the townland
That is the world's bane.'

When their hearts are so high
That they would come to blows,
They unhook their heavy swords
From golden and silver boughs;
But all that are killed in battle
Awaken to life again.
It is lucky that their story
Is not known among men,
For O, the strong farmers
That would let the spade lie,
Their hearts would be like a cup
That somebody had drunk dry.

The little fox he murmured,
'O what of the world's bane?'
The sun was laughing sweetly,
The moon plucked at my rein;
But the little red fox murmured,
'O do not pluck at his rein,
He is riding to the townland
That is the world's bane.'

Michael will unhook his trumpet
From a bough overhead,
And blow a little noise
When the supper has been spread.
Gabriel will come from the water
With a fish-tail, and talk
Of wonders that have happened
On wet roads where men walk,
And lift up an old horn
Of hammered silver, and drink
Till he has fallen asleep
Upon the starry brink.

The little fox he murmured,
'O what of the world's bane?'
The sun was laughing sweetly,
The moon plucked at my rein;
But the little red fox murmured,
'O do not pluck at his rein,
He is riding to the townland
That is the world's bane.'

There was a stage-play by Yeats written in prose and entitled *The Golden Helmet*, then rewritten in verse and retitled *The Green Helmet*, and published along with a set of twenty-one poems, a few of which we print here. For several reasons they are fascinating.

The poet had by that time suffered, and survived, the shock and disillusion caused by the marriage of Maud Gonne to Major John MacBride, soldier from the absurdity of the South African war returning (but then what war is not absurd?), in which he had fought for the Boers.

The sister of Thomas MacDonagh, a venerable nun when, in her later years, she talked to me, told me that the marriage was simply the result of hero-worship. But she was prepared to admit that the disillusioned poet might have been pardoned for viewing it otherwise.

Of the poems written in that mood, and around that period, Norman Jeffares writes:

His genuinely romantic poetry had come to a stop. Once she was married there was nothing to look forward to, even with diminishing hope. The puzzle to him had been that, when they went to see the Lia Fail, Maud had appeared to understand his plans, especially those for the Castle of the Heroes, to be built of Irish stone and decorated with the four jewels of the Tuatha de Danaan, with perhaps a statue of Ireland. The Lia Fail corresponded with the Altar, and the other symbols were the Cauldron of the Dagda, the Golden Spear of Victory of Lugh, and the Sword of Light. It seemed impossible to him that she could not marry him, knowing his love and his plans for Ireland. Her marriage carried conviction that all hope of achieving the loveliness of his dreams was gone, and so there is an air of finality about the love-poetry written after 1903.

There were the inevitable commentators who feared that because the poems were changing, the poet might have written himself out. With our sapient hindsight we know that this was not the case, and the following poems show how wise we would have been had we said so in 1910.

One of my favourite quotations from the poet comes from the end of the play *The Green Helmet*, when the mysterious Red Man from the Sea crowns Cuchulain as the bravest of the heroes, and gives the reason for his choice:

> *And I choose the laughing lip*
> *That shall not turn from laughing, whatever rise or fall;*
> *The heart that grows no bitterer, although betrayed by all;*
> *The hand that loves to scatter; the life like a gambler's*
> *   throw;*
> *And these things I make prosper, till a day come that I*
> *   know,*
> *When heart and mind shall darken that the weak may end*
> *   the strong,*
> *And the long-remembering harpers have matter for their*
> *   song.*

MAUD GONNE
by Sarah Purser
(1848–1943).

NO SECOND TROY

Why should I blame her that she filled my days
With misery, or that she would of late
Have taught to ignorant men most violent ways,
Or hurled the little streets upon the great,
Had they but courage equal to desire?
What could have made her peaceful with a mind
That nobleness made simple as a fire,
With beauty like a tightened bow, a kind
That is not natural in an age like this,
Being high and solitary and most stern?
Why, what could she have done, being what she is?
Was there another Troy for her to burn?

ALL THINGS CAN TEMPT ME

All things can tempt me from this craft of verse:
One time it was a woman's face, or worse —
The seeming needs of my fool-driven land;
Now nothing but comes readier to the hand
Than this accustomed toil. When I was young,
I had not given a penny for a song
Did not the poet sing it with such airs
That one believed he had a sword upstairs;
Yet would be now, could I but have my wish,
Colder and dumber and deafer than a fish.

UPON A HOUSE SHAKEN BY THE LAND AGITATION

How should the world be luckier if this house,
Where passion and precision have been one
Time out of mind, became too ruinous
To breed the lidless eye that loves the sun?
And the sweet laughing eagle thoughts that grow
Where wings have memory of wings, and all
That comes of the best knit to the best? Although
Mean roof-trees were the sturdier for its fall,
How should their luck run high enough to reach
The gifts that govern men, and after these
To gradual Time's last gift, a written speech
Wrought of high laughter, loveliness and ease?

The ghost of Moore Hall, County Mayo,
ancestral home of George Moore, the novelist.

There where the course is,
Delight makes all of the one mind,
The riders upon the galloping horses,
The crowd that closes in behind:
We, too, had good attendance once,
Hearers and hearteners of the work;
Aye, horsemen for companions,
Before the merchant and the clerk
Breathed on the world with timid breath.
Sing on: somewhere at some new moon,
We'll learn that sleeping is not death.
Hearing the whole earth change its tune,
Its flesh being wild, and it again
Crying aloud as the racecourse is,
And we find hearteners among men
That ride upon horses.

THE RACE DAY, *1912, by Jack B. Yeats.*

THE RACE DAY

RESPONSIBILITIES 1914

In dreams begins responsibility.   OLD PLAY

How am I fallen from myself, for a long time now
I have not seen the Prince of Chang in my dreams.
                                KHOUNG-FOU-TSEU

THE CUALA PRESS
CHURCHTOWN
DUNDRUM
MCMXIV

In the dedicatory poem to this collection, 'Pardon, old fathers' (p. 64), T. S. Eliot sensed, not without reason, a certain anguish. The poet is, admittedly, asking pardon for not having, what the language of advertising might now call, 'achieved': as a man of action, perhaps, and a begetter of sons. He had claimed, with what we may well regard as excessive humility, nothing but a book to prove his claim to be of his ancestors' blood and bone, and he may at times have felt that – like his own creation in his tales of the poet, Red Hanrahan – he had been astray in an enchanted wilderness.

Yet there is also in these lines an obvious and notable resonant pride in a dignified, honourable history and ancestry, mounting up to that statement about the wasteful virtues that earn the sun. The Red Man from the Sea could again, as in *The Green Helmet*, be showing his preference for the laughing lip that shall not turn from laughing, whatever rise or fall.

Pride in ancestors, whether we have had them or not, and I sincerely hope you do not misunderstand me, is something many of us are inclined to indulge in, and it may easily expose us to the gibes of the unsympathetic. George Moore, the novelist – and in many ways, and from what I have heard from some people who knew him, a perfect gentleman – was, nevertheless, not found wanting at that game. Yet it is obvious that the poet had in his ancestry much to be proud of.

From the shades of his ancestors Yeats turns to salute the shades of those poets with whom he claimed that, in a tavern in London – long ago associated with Samuel Johnson and Edmund Burke and, above all, Oliver Goldsmith – 'sipping at the honeypot of his mind', he had learned his trade, this craft of verse.

For their sake he remakes an old tale from the heroic times, and from the enchanted mountain of Sliabh na mBan, the Mountain of the Women, in County Tipperary; and it is, perhaps, a permissible fantasy to think of Yeats, standing on the summit of that noble mountain and casting his story like a spell towards mighty and multitudinous London. He is also looking from the ancient past into his own past and, for the moment, and to be even more fantastic, putting the present and the future behind him.

In 'The Grey Rock' (p. 64), of those companions of the Cheshire Cheese the poet mentions only Ernest Dowson and Lionel Johnson. T. W. Rolleston, the Irishman who wrote one fine poem, 'The Dead at Clonmacnois', might, better than the other two, have appreciated the tale. But Yeats and Rolleston, in their various efforts to create a new Ireland, had had their little differences.

We must remember that by now Yeats had well proved himself a great poet, that he had founded a theatre, that with style and courage and, at times, with a rage that would have done credit to old Grandfather Pollexfen (who leaped into salt water to rescue an airborne, seaborne hat), he had faced up to the controversy over that theatre, over the destiny of the celebrated collection of paintings that Sir Hugh Lane, the nephew of Lady Gregory, had wished to offer to the city of Dublin. And over other matters.

He had become a public man, but not yet a smiling public man, as much later he was, with some irony and some sadness, to describe himself.

The row in Dublin over the Lane pictures was unpleasant and had long-lasting echoes. Lane, an art-dealer of the highest order, had assembled a distinguished collection of modern French paintings and was prepared to give them to Dublin city if a fitting gallery were found or built in which to house them. There were various plans, including a most imaginative submission by Sir Edwin Lutyens, for building a bridge-gallery across the Liffey where the Ha'penny Bridge spans the translucent stream. Plans! But not enough money with which to carry them out.

Arguments began. In Dublin, as anywhere else, one argument is liable to become entangled with another, and one word spoken idly gives birth to twenty words

spoken with venom. Lane, in a perhaps comprehensible temper, gave the pictures to London, then changed his mind – and his will – again, but sank in the *Lusitania* tragedy before the altered will could be witnessed.

Lord Ardilaun, it seems, was the wealthy man of Yeats' poem (p. 68) who wondered if the people really wanted pictures. William Martin Murphy, a notable and formidable proprietor of newspapers and transport companies, may have thought that the reproof was intended for him: he was already an enemy of Yeats.

Out of such odd, and even absurd, occasions great poetry can be born.

Those were turbulent years in Dublin. The Labour agitation, led by the great James Larkin, was, in 1913, to stand up to the offensive of a lockout for which that same William Martin Murphy was mainly responsible. Politics, with the obviously forthcoming collapse of the Home Rule Movement, was heating up towards the armed revolution against British rule, of Easter 1916. In the north-east of the country, Edward Carson, briefed by the High Tories, had defied what might have been laughingly described as democracy and, as Helen Waddell said, 'practically created Sinn Féin'.

The streets of Dublin city, and the roads of Ireland, were bitter with memories of the betrayal by politicians (English and Irish) and by bishops (Irish) of the uncrowned King of Ireland, Charles Stewart Parnell, a magnificent and tragic figure who has haunted our memory and imagination, from Yeats and James Joyce down to this present day.

There is sadness, and a white anger, in the poems of this period.

In 'September 1913' (p. 68) the poet mourns the death of John O'Leary, that noble figure, the old Fenian revolutionary who had inspired Yeats' revolutionary years. He contrasts O'Leary's nobility and, as he sees it, that of the reckless and doomed patriots of the past, Lord Edward Fitzgerald, Robert Emmet and Wolfe Tone, 'All that delirium of the brave', with a pious, craven, money-grubbing section of Ireland which he elected to see in the present.

Every honest Irishman, to this day, will respond to his words. But in 'September 1913' Yeats was most certainly unjust to a lot of decent people. Who felt hurt. And those whom he was really describing would have remained, as such people always do, and as he was well aware, unscathed.

In 'To a Friend Whose Work Has Come to Nothing' (p. 72) Yeats said he was speaking to Lady Gregory. About whom, we do not seem to be quite certain. But when, in 'To a Shade' (p. 72), he speaks to another shade, or ghost, there is no doubt but that he is speaking most solemnly to the people of Ireland, and that he is assured that the echo of his words may well be heard on the Other Island: not the Other Island that Bernard Shaw, at the request of William Yeats, wrote about in a comic and wise play.

All the arguments and angers of that time come together in this sombre and, to this day, quite disturbing poem. There may always be, in any great city, ghosts to be seen walking the streets, and it may be that legend and poetry preserve them and remind us, for ever, that they still walk. But few ghosts can have had such honour paid to them as Yeats, in this great poem, paid to Charles Stewart Parnell: seeing him, in sombre vision, walking forth from Glasnevin cemetery, in the north of Dublin city, where so many of the patriotic, and other, dead lie together. There too the last and badly needed resting-place of Parnell is marked by a circle of small trees and an inner circle of smooth grass concentrating on one simple, impressive piece of Wicklow granite, bearing only one word: Parnell.

The man of Parnell's own passionate, serving kind was Hugh Lane. The 'old foul mouth' compliment was, most likely, meant for William Martin Murphy, although I have heard it argued, by men older and wiser than myself, that the poet may also have been thinking of the famous and sharp-tongued parliamentarian Timothy Healy. Peace be to all their ghosts!

The most intense confrontation between the poet and some of the people of Ireland came when John Millington Synge wrote for the stage of the Abbey Theatre *The Playboy of the Western World*, based on a story, the glimmerings of which came to Synge on the Aran Islands, whither he had gone at the suggestion of Yeats.

Some Irish nationalists, in the theatre audience and in the popular press, confronted with the strange tale of the wandering young man who thought he had killed his father in an almost reasonable act of self-defence (and who became a popular hero because of the distant and glorified prospect of that 'gallous deed') thought that, in the very telling of such a tale, the Irish national character had been befouled. Also, some simple puritans reacted against the use on the stage of some simple, domestic words. The result was an uproarious row, and the difficult delivery of a masterpiece which, thanks to the man who wrote it and the players who played in it, and the man who nourished and defended it, is one of our most priceless national possessions. Yeats' response came in 'On Those That Hated "The Playboy of the Western World"' (p. 70).

Later the poet speaks, somewhere on the Irish shore, 'To a Child Dancing in the Wind' (p. 74) and envies that youth; he mourns in 'Two Years Later' (p. 74), as he is to do with increasing anger, the relentless advance of age. But youth and innocence he knows, as we all do with the passing of time, are fragile and transient, and from those two poems to the young Iseult he returns to record once again his memory of the majesty of her mother, Maud, and to think of the heedless people in the streets who may neither know nor care that such a wonder once passed that way (p. 74).

W.B. YEATS AND THE IRISH THEATRE, *1915,*
by Edmund Dulac (1882–1953).

Pardon, old fathers, if you still remain
Somewhere in ear-shot for the story's end,
Old Dublin merchant 'free of the ten and four'
Or trading out of Galway into Spain;
Old country scholar, Robert Emmet's friend,
A hundred-year-old memory to the poor;
Merchant and scholar who have left me blood
That has not passed through any huckster's loin,
Soldiers that gave, whatever die was cast:
A Butler or an Armstrong that withstood
Beside the brackish waters of the Boyne
James and his Irish when the Dutchman crossed;
Old merchant skipper that leaped overboard
After a ragged hat in Biscay Bay;
You most of all, silent and fierce old man,
Because the daily spectacle that stirred
My fancy, and set my boyish lips to say,
'Only the wasteful virtues earn the sun';
Pardon that for a barren passion's sake,
Although I have come close on forty-nine,
I have no child, I have nothing but a book,
Nothing but that to prove your blood and mine.

January 1914

THE GREY ROCK

Poets with whom I learned my trade,
Companions of the Cheshire Cheese,
Here's an old story I've remade,
Imagining 'twould better please
Your ears than stories now in fashion,
Though you may think I waste my breath
Pretending that there can be passion
That has more life in it than death,
And though at bottling of your wine
Old wholesome Goban had no say;
The moral's yours because it's mine.

When cups went round at close of day –
Is not that how good stories run? –
The gods were sitting at the board
In their great house at Slievenamon.
They sang a drowsy song, or snored,
For all were full of wine and meat.
The smoky torches made a glare
On metal Goban 'd hammered at,
On old deep silver rolling there
Or on some still unemptied cup
That he, when frenzy stirred his thews,
Had hammered out on mountain top
To hold the sacred stuff he brews
That only gods may buy of him.
Now from that juice that made them wise
All those had lifted up the dim
Imaginations of their eyes,
For one that was like woman made
Before their sleepy eyelids ran
And trembling with her passion said,
'Come out and dig for a dead man,
Who's burrowing somewhere in the ground,
And mock him to his face and then
Hollo him on with horse and hound,
For he is the worst of all dead men.'

We should be dazed and terror-struck,
If we but saw in dreams that room,
Those wine-drenched eyes, and curse our luck
That emptied all our days to come.
I knew a woman none could please,
Because she dreamed when but a child
Of men and women made like these;
And after, when her blood ran wild,
Had ravelled her own story out,
And said, 'In two or in three years
I needs must marry some poor lout,'
And having said it, burst in tears.

Since, tavern comrades, you have died,
Maybe your images have stood,
Mere bone and muscle thrown aside,
Before that roomful or as good.
You had to face your ends when young —
'Twas wine or women, or some curse —
But never made a poorer song.
That you might have a heavier purse,
Nor gave loud service to a cause
That you might have a troop of friends.
You kept the Muses' sterner laws,
And unrepenting faced your ends,
And therefore earned the right — and yet
Dowson and Johnson most I praise —
To troop with those the world's forgot,
And copy their proud steady gaze.

'The Danish troop was driven out
Between the dawn and dusk,' she said;
'Although the event was long in doubt,
Although the King of Ireland's dead
And half the kings, before sundown
All was accomplished.
                              'When this day
Murrough, the King of Ireland's son,
Foot after foot was giving way,
He and his best troops back to back
Had perished there, but the Danes ran,
Stricken with panic from the attack,
The shouting of an unseen man;
And being thankful Murrough found,
Led by a footsole dipped in blood
That had made prints upon the ground,
Where by old thorn-trees that man stood;
And though when he gazed here and there,
He had but gazed on thorn-trees, spoke,
"Who is the friend that seems but air
And yet could give so fine a stroke?"
Thereon a young man met his eye,
Who said, "Because she held me in
Her love, and would not have me die,
Rock-nurtured Aoife took a pin,
And pushing it into my shirt,
Promised that for a pin's sake
No man should see to do me hurt;
But there it's gone; I will not take
The fortune that had been my shame
Seeing, King's son, what wounds you have."
'Twas roundly spoke, but when night came

He had betrayed me to his grave,
For he and the King's son were dead.
I'd promised him two hundred years,
And when for all I'd done or said —
And these immortal eyes shed tears —
He claimed his country's need was most,
I'd saved his life, yet for the sake
Of a new friend he has turned a ghost.
What does he care if my heart break?
I call for spade and horse and hound
That we may harry him.' Thereon
She cast herself upon the ground
And rent her clothes and made her moan:
'Why are they faithless when their might
Is from the holy shades that rove
The grey rock and the windy light?
Why should the faithfullest heart most love
The bitter sweetness of false faces?
Why must the lasting love what passes,
Why are the gods by men betrayed?'

But thereon every god stood up
With a slow smile and without sound,
And stretching forth his arm and cup
To where she moaned upon the ground,
Suddenly drenched her to the skin;
And she with Goban's wine adrip,
No more remembering what had been,
Stared at the gods with laughing lip.

I have kept my faith, though faith was tried,
To that rock-born, rock-wandering foot,
And the world's altered since you died,
And I am in no good repute
With the loud host before the sea,
That think sword-strokes were better meant
Than lover's music — let that be,
So that the wandering foot's content.

(Left) '... silent and fierce old man',
William Pollexfen, the poet's grandfather.

(Overleaf) Truskmore, in the Sligo-Leitrim range,
near neighbour of Glenade, the Hag's Leap,
Ben-Weeskin, and bare Ben Bulben.

TO A WEALTHY MAN
WHO PROMISED A SECOND SUBSCRIPTION
TO THE DUBLIN MUNICIPAL GALLERY
IF IT WERE PROVED THE PEOPLE
WANTED PICTURES

You gave, but will not give again
Until enough of Paudeen's pence
By Biddy's halfpennies have lain
To be 'some sort of evidence',
Before you'll put your guineas down,
That things it were a pride to give
Are what the blind and ignorant town
Imagines best to make it thrive.
What cared Duke Ercole, that bid
His mummers to the market-place,
What th' onion-sellers thought or did
So that his Plautus set the pace
For the Italian comedies?
And Guidobaldo, when he made
That grammer school of courtesies
Where wit and beauty learned their trade
Upon Urbino's windy hill,
Had sent no runners to and fro
That he might learn the shepherds' will.
And when they drove out Cosimo,
Indifferent how the rancour ran,
He gave the hours they had set free
To Michelozzo's latest plan
For the San Marco Library,
Whence turbulent Italy should draw
Delight in Art whose end is peace,
In logic and in natural law
By sucking at the dugs of Greece.

Your open hand but shows our loss,
For he knew better how to live.
Let Paudeens play at pitch and toss,
Look up in the sun's eye and give
What the exultant heart calls good
That some new day may breed the best
Because you gave, not what they would,
But the right twigs for an eagle's nest!

December 1912

SEPTEMBER 1913

What need you, being come to sense,
But fumble in a greasy till
And add the halfpence to the pence
And prayer to shivering prayer, until
You have dried the marrow from the bone?
For men were born to pray and save:
Romantic Ireland's dead and gone,
It's with O'Leary in the grave.

Yet they were of a different kind,
The names that stilled your childish play,
They have gone about the world like wind,
But little time had they to pray
For whom the hangman's rope was spun,
And what, God help us, could they save?
Romantic Ireland's dead and gone,
It's with O'Leary in the grave.

Was it for this the wild geese spread
The grey wing upon every tide;
For this that all that blood was shed,
For this Edward Fitzgerald died,
And Robert Emmet and Wolfe Tone,
All that delirium of the brave?
Romantic Ireland's dead and gone,
It's with O'Leary in the grave.

Yet could we turn the years again,
And call those exiles as they were
In all their loneliness and pain,
You'd cry, 'Some woman's yellow hair
Has maddened every mother's son':
They weighed so lightly what they gave.
But let them be, they're dead and gone,
They're with O'Leary in the grave.

Sold by the Irish Players at $1.00 towards a building to save Sir Hugh Lane's Great Gift of Pictures for Ireland April 1913

Look up in the sun's eye, and give
What the exalted heart calls good,
That some new day may breed the best,
Because you gave, not what they would,
But the right twigs for an eagle's nest.

"Michael Cooney: Where is the use of calling it a lend, when I
know I never will see it again? It might as well earn me
the value of a charity."

*A linen handkerchief sold for a dollar to raise funds
to house Hugh Lane's picture collection in Dublin.
The eight Abbey players at the bottom, from
sketches by John Butler Yeats, are: (top row)
Arthur Sinclair, Sara Allgood, Eithne Magee,
Sydney J. Morgan; (bottom row) J.A.O'Rourke,
J.M.Kerrigan, Udolphus Wright, Fred O'Donovan.*

ON THOSE THAT HATED
'THE PLAYBOY OF THE WESTERN WORLD', 1907

Once, when midnight smote the air,
Eunuchs ran through Hell and met
On every crowded street to stare
Upon great Juan riding by:
Even like these to rail and sweat
Staring upon his sinewy thigh.

*Yeats addresses the audience from the stage of the
Abbey Theatre.*
*'I never witnessed a human being fight as Yeats
fought that night, nor knew another with so many
weapons in his armoury,' wrote Mary Colum.*

THE ABBEY ROW.

NOT Edited by W. B. YEATS.

JOHN MILLINGTON SYNGE *by John Butler Yeats,*
author of The Playboy of the Western World.

TO A FRIEND WHOSE WORK
HAS COME TO NOTHING

Now all the truth is out,
Be secret and take defeat
From any brazen throat,
For how can you compete,
Being honour bred, with one
Who, were it proved he lies,
Were neither shamed in his own
Nor in his neighbours' eyes?
Bred to a harder thing
Than Triumph, turn away
And like a laughing string
Whereon mad fingers play
Amid a place of stone,
Be secret and exult,
Because of all things known
That is most difficult.

TO A SHADE

If you have revisited the town, thin Shade,
Whether to look upon your monument
(I wonder if the builder has been paid)
Or happier-thoughted when the day is spent
To drink of that salt breath out of the sea
When grey gulls flit about instead of men,
And the gaunt houses put on majesty:
Let these content you and be gone again:
For they are at their old tricks yet.
                                        A man
Of your own passionate serving kind who had brought
In his full hands what, had they only known,
Had given their children's children loftier thought,
Sweeter emotion, working in their veins
Like gentle blood, has been driven from the place,
And insult heaped upon him for his pains.
And for his open-handedness, disgrace;
Your enemy, an old foul mouth, had set
The pack upon him.
                            Go, unquiet wanderer,
And gather the Glasnevin coverlet
About your head till the dust stops your ear,
The time for you to taste of that salt breath
And listen at the corners has not come:
You had enough of sorrow before death —
Away, away! You are safer in the tomb.

September 29, 1913

(Above) Charles Stewart Parnell (1846–91), and Kitty O'Shea.

(Right) Parnell speaks from a window in the Victoria Hotel in the main street of Cork City, as James Larkin is later to do from a hotel window in the main street of Dublin.

MR. PARNELL ADDRESSING HIS CONSTITUENTS FROM A WINDOW OF THE VICTORIA HOTEL AT CORK.

73

I

TO A CHILD DANCING IN THE WIND

Dance there upon the shore;
What need have you to care
For wind or water's roar?
And tumble out your hair
That the salt drops have wet;
Being young you have not known
The fool's triumph, nor yet
Love lost as soon as won,
Nor the best labourer dead
And all the sheaves to bind.
What need have you to dread
The monstrous crying of wind?

II

TWO YEARS LATER

Has no one said those daring
Kind eyes should be more learn'd?
Or warned you how despairing
The moths are when they are burned?
I could have warned you; but you are young,
So we speak a different tongue.

O you will take whatever's offered
And dream that all the world's a friend,
Suffer as your mother suffered,
Be as broken in the end.
But I am old and you are young,
And I speak a barbarous tongue.

FALLEN MAJESTY

Although crowds gathered once if she but showed her face,
And even old men's eyes grew dim, this hand alone,
Like some last courtier at a gypsy camping-place
Babbling of fallen majesty, records what's gone.

The lineaments, a heart that laughter has made sweet,
These, these remain, but I record what's gone. A crowd
Will gather, and not know it walks the very street
Whereon a thing once walked that seemed a burning cloud.

THE WILD SWANS AT COOLE 1919

The poet grows old and the events of his own life and the spectacle of the world around him have left him much to brood on. He walks by the lake shore near the great house of Coole, where he has found invaluable friendship and an ease of mind in the sight of a pattern of life, ordered and gracious. Nineteen years have passed since he first made his count of the swans on the water (p. 78).

The poet, Blind Antony Raftery, lamenting the death of the piper, Thomás Ó Dálaigh, had said something like this: 'Tall swans on the water are as black as the fruit on the thorn since the man slipped away from us who had merriment on the tips of his fingers.' From Douglas Hyde who edited, with copious commentary, the poems and songs of Raftery, Yeats may have heard a lot about the blind poet; and that image of the swans losing their whiteness because of the death of a great musician would have struck a chord.

The beauty of the swans' shape, their legendary agelessness, their fabled fidelity, lover to lover, their seasonal departure, leaping 'into the desolate heaven', their faithful return – all those things have, for as long as we know, transformed the swan into a sacred bird.

Frank O'Connor used to argue, with a certain amount of conscious paradox to which that most amiable man was somewhat given, that Yeats was even more notably the poet of friendship than the celebrant of the love of man for woman. Paradox? Yet there is so much in Yeats to support O'Connor's argument:

Think where man's glory most begins and ends,
And say my glory was I had such friends.

After his marriage, in 1917, to George Hyde-Lees,

Yeats picked for what we may call a central and symbolic home the ancient stone tower, at a bridge over a small river, at Ballylee. It was in the neighbourhood of Lady Gregory's Coole and Edward Martyn's Tulira, and the crossroads of Kiltartan where Blind Raftery had sung that he had encountered the beauty, Mary Hynes; and near King Guaire's Gort out of which, you might say, came the legend of Yeats' play *The King's Threshold*.

That tower was also, as we shall see, to signify to Yeats that the Ireland he had envisioned could have been, should have been, to a great extent founded on and shaped by the minds of those giants of the eighteenth century: Jonathan Swift, Edmund Burke, Oliver Goldsmith, Henry Grattan, and the philosopher, George Berkeley, Bishop of Cloyne, who on a certain matter of philosophical dispute said, 'We Irish think otherwise.'

So the poet speaks to his wife and says that always we would have the new friend meet the old, and he welcomes to the ancient tower the shadows of dead friends – Lionel Johnson, John Synge – and mourns that the discourtesy of death, most discourteous in days of war, should have taken away his friend (and the son of his friend), Robert Gregory (p. 80).

Then he turns in 'The Fisherman' (p. 84) to the image of the tall, tweed-clothed man, fishing-rod in hand, climbing the mountainside to drop the fly in pools in the mountain streams. My own feeling is that the man would have fared better with live bait on a Stewart tackle: but that is a mere technical detail. For that was the sort of man the poet had always wished to be, ever since, as a shy and sensitive young fellow, he had climbed Ben Bulben's back and had the 'livelong summer day to spend'.

Yet the ghost of his lost passion follows Yeats and he

pays tribute to it in what seem to me to be three of his finest poems, 'Her Praise' (p. 84), 'Broken Dreams' (p. 85) and 'His Phoenix' (p. 86).

Any commentary would be an impertinence. Dylan Thomas said, wisely enough, that when reading poetry you should read until you find what you like and then read it again. Preferably, I might add, read it aloud, with or without an audience. The angels will hear you.

You might say that Yeats felt that that symbolic house, the tower at Ballylee, was growing like a garment around him and re-creating a past, and a century, to his own idea of which he was to become more and more devoted. In 'A Prayer on Going into My House' (p. 87) he prays for a blessing on the tower and on the simple cottage beside and below it, and on those who may follow him to live in that simplicity, and touch and handle those plain objects that the great and passionate may have touched and handled in the past. Historical continuity by way of domestic utensil! It is not as naive as it may seem to some of us in this era of planned obsolescence.

But the doorway of the tower is not to be closed on vision and wonder and, should the outside world intrude, the poet is prepared to bestow on it a quite classical curse.

The last poem in this collection, 'The Double Vision of Michael Robartes' (p. 88), brings us into those obscure highways, or byways, that Yeats may first have followed in the company of George Russell and some others.

As far away as the hoarse Trinacrian shore of Oregon, a fine young woman, a university student, told me, exactly twenty-two years ago, that she was beginning to read W. B. Yeats. This pleased me very much and I asked her what of Yeats she was wrestling with.

She said she was beginning with *A Vision*, that highly difficult prose-work in which the poet, struggling, as always, towards truth, attempts to work out from observation of the world and the ways of men, of the universe, the moon and the sun, and from strange spiritual revelations (not excluding automatic writing) a system that would relate to and illuminate human history, the varieties and types of men and the soul and destiny of man.

Most humbly I suggested that *A Vision* might not be the easiest point of attack on the fortifications that Yeats quite frequently seems to build up against any facile interpretation. But the brave, undaunted young woman seemed quite happy with her discovery and her comprehension.

Some years later she was married and the ceremony was held under the sky and on that wild shore of the Pacific somewhere in the neighbourhood of Coos Bay: an idea that would most certainly have pleased the poet. Or did she take the idea from his words to the girl dancing on the shore?

Regardless of all that, I still would feel uneasy about recommending *A Vision* as the first work of Yeats that anybody should or could read. But here, with 'The Double Vision of Michael Robartes', would seem to me to be a point of attack. Where in Ireland but on ancient Cashel of the Kings, Cormac's Cashel, would we find a more fitting sanctuary for visions and dreams?

Read the poem and re-read it. Then consider such early prose works as *Rosa Alchemica, The Tables of the Law, and The Adoration of the Magi* (1897) and *Per Amica Silentia Lunae* (1917).

The trees are in their autumn beauty,
The woodland paths are dry,
Under the October twilight the water
Mirrors a still sky;
Upon the brimming water among the stones
Are nine-and-fifty swans.

The nineteenth autumn has come upon me
Since I first made my count;
I saw, before I had well finished,
All suddenly mount
And scatter wheeling in great broken rings
Upon their clamorous wings.

I have looked upon those brilliant creatures,
And now my heart is sore.
All's changed since I, hearing at twilight,
The first time on this shore,
The bell-beat of their wings above my head,
Trod with a lighter tread.

Unwearied still, lover by lover,
They paddle in the cold
Companionable streams or climb the air;
Their hearts have not grown old;
Passion or conquest, wander where they will,
Attend upon them still.

But now they drift on the still water,
Mysterious, beautiful;
Among what rushes will they build,
By what lake's edge or pool
Delight men's eyes when I awake some day
To find they have flown away?

I

Now that we're almost settled in our house
I'll name the friends that cannot sup with us
Beside a fire of turf in th' ancient tower,
And having talked to some late hour
Climb up the narrow winding stair to bed:
Discoverers of forgotten truth
Or mere companions of my youth,
All, all are in my thoughts to-night being dead.

II

Always we'd have the new friend meet the old
And we are hurt if either friend seem cold,
And there is salt to lengthen out the smart
In the affections of our heart,
And quarrels are blown up upon that head;
But not a friend that I would bring
This night can set us quarrelling,
For all that come into my mind are dead.

III

Lionel Johnson comes the first to mind,
That loved his learning better than mankind,
Though courteous to the worst; much falling he
Brooded upon sanctity
Till all his Greek and Latin learning seemed
A long blast upon the horn that brought
A little nearer to his thought
A measureless consummation that he dreamed.

IV

And that enquiring man John Synge comes next,
That dying chose the living world for text
And never could have rested in the tomb
But that, long travelling, he had come
Towards nightfall upon certain set apart
In a most desolate stony place,
Towards nightfall upon a race
Passionate and simple like his heart.

V

And then I think of old George Pollexfen,
In muscular youth well known to Mayo men
For horsemanship at meets or at racecourses,
That could have shown how pure-bred horses
And solid men, for all their passion, live
But as the outrageous stars incline
By opposition, square and trine;
Having grown sluggish and contemplative.

VI

They were my close companions many a year,
A portion of my mind and life, as it were,
And now their breathless faces seem to look
Out of some old picture-book;
I am accustomed to their lack of breath,
But not that my dear friend's dear son,
Our Sidney and our perfect man,
Could share in that discourtesy of death.

VII

For all things the delighted eye now sees
Were loved by him: the old storm-broken trees
That cast their shadows upon road and bridge;
The tower set on the stream's edge;
The ford where drinking cattle make a stir
Nightly, and startled by that sound
The water-hen must change her ground;
He might have been your heartiest welcomer.

VIII

When with the Galway foxhounds he would ride
From Castle Taylor to the Roxborough side
Or Esserkelly plain, few kept his pace;
At Mooneen he had leaped a place
So perilous that half the astonished meet
Had shut their eyes; and where was it
He rode a race without a bit?
And yet his mind outran the horses' feet.

IX

We dreamed that a great painter had been born
To cold Clare rock and Galway rock and thorn,
To that stern colour and that delicate line
That are our secret discipline
Wherein the gazing heart doubles her might.
Soldier, scholar, horseman, he,
And yet he had the intensity
To have published all to be a world's delight.

X

What other could so well have counselled us
In all lovely intricacies of a house
As he that practised or that understood
All work in metal or in wood,
In moulded plaster or in carven stone?
Soldier, scholar, horseman, he,
And all he did done perfectly
As though he had but that one trade alone.

XI

Some burn damp faggots, others may consume
The entire combustible world in one small room
As though dried straw, and if we turn about
The bare chimney is gone black out
Because the work had finished in that flare.
Soldier, scholar, horseman, he,
As 'twere all life's epitome.
What made us dream that he could comb grey hair?

XII

I had thought, seeing how bitter is that wind
That shakes the shutter, to have brought to mind
All those that manhood tried, or childhood loved
Or boyish intellect approved,
With some appropriate commentary on each;
Until imagination brought
A fitter welcome; but a thought
Of that late death took all my heart for speech.

A sketch by Jack B. Yeats of Robert Gregory on Sarsfield at the Gort Show, 1906.

AN IRISH AIRMAN FORESEES HIS DEATH

I know that I shall meet my fate
Somewhere among the clouds above;
Those that I fight I do not hate,
Those that I guard I do not love;
My country is Kiltartan Cross,
My countrymen Kiltartan's poor,
No likely end could bring them loss
Or leave them happier than before.
Nor law, nor duty bade me fight,
Nor public men, nor cheering crowds,
A lonely impulse of delight
Drove to this tumult in the clouds;
I balanced all, brought all to mind,
The years to come seemed waste of breath,
A waste of breath the years behind
In balance with this life, this death.

ROBERT GREGORY *by Charles Shannon (1863–1937).*

Although I can see him still,
The freckled man who goes
To a grey place on a hill
In grey Connemara clothes
At dawn to cast his flies,
It's long since I began
To call up to the eyes
This wise and simple man.
All day I'd looked in the face
What I had hoped 'twould be
To write for my own race
And the reality;
The living men that I hate,
The dead man that I loved,
The craven man in his seat,
The insolent unreproved,
And no knave brought to book
Who has won a drunken cheer,
The witty man and his joke
Aimed at the commonest ear,
The clever man who cries
The catch-cries of the clown,
The beating down of the wise
And great Art beaten down.

Maybe a twelvemonth since
Suddenly I began,
In scorn of this audience,
Imagining a man,
And his sun-freckled face,
And grey Connemara cloth,
Climbing up to a place
Where stone is dark under froth,
And the down-turn of his wrist
When the flies drop in the stream;
A man who does not exist,
A man who is but a dream;
And cried, 'Before I am old
I shall have written him one
Poem maybe as cold
And passionate as the dawn.'

She is foremost of those that I would hear praised.
I have gone about the house, gone up and down
As a man does who has published a new book,
Or a young girl dressed out in her new gown,
And though I have turned the talk by hook or crook
Until her praise should be the uppermost theme,
A woman spoke of some new tale she had read,
A man confusedly in a half dream
As though some other name ran in his head.
She is foremost of those that I would hear praised.
I will talk no more of books or the long war
But walk by the dry thorn until I have found
Some beggar sheltering from the wind, and there
Manage the talk until her name come round.
If there be rags enough he will know her name
And be well pleased remembering it, for in the old days,
Though she had young men's praise and old men's blame,
Among the poor both old and young gave her praise.

BROKEN DREAMS

There is grey in your hair.
Young men no longer suddenly catch their breath
When you are passing;
But maybe some old gaffer mutters a blessing
Because it was your prayer
Recovered him upon the bed of death.
For your sole sake – that all heart's ache have known,
And given to others all heart's ache,
From meagre girlhood's putting on
Burdensome beauty – for your sole sake
Heaven has put away the stroke of her doom,
So great her portion in that peace you make
By merely walking in a room.

Your beauty can but leave among us
Vague memories, nothing but memories.
A young man when the old men are done talking
Will say to an old man, 'Tell me of that lady
The poet stubborn with his passion sang us
When age might well have chilled his blood.'

Vague memories, nothing but memories,
But in the grave all, all, shall be renewed.
The certainty that I shall see that lady
Leaning or standing or walking
In the first loveliness of womanhood,
And with the fervour of my youthful eyes,
Has set me muttering like a fool.

You are more beautiful than any one,
And yet your body had a flaw:
Your small hands were not beautiful,
And I am afraid that you will run
And paddle to the wrist
In that mysterious, always brimming lake
Where those that have obeyed the holy law
Paddle and are perfect. Leave unchanged
The hands that I have kissed,
For old sake's sake.

The last stroke of midnight dies.
All day in the one chair
From dream to dream and rhyme to rhyme I have ranged
In rambling talk with an image of air:
Vague memories, nothing but memories.

MAUD GONNE MACBRIDE *(Madame MacBride),*
1929, by Seán O'Sullivan (1906–64).

There is a queen in China, or maybe it's in Spain,
And birthdays and holidays such praises can be heard
Of her unblemished lineaments, a whiteness with no stain,
That she might be that sprightly girl trodden by a bird;
And there's a score of duchesses, surpassing womankind,
Or who have found a painter to make them so for pay
And smooth out stain and blemish with the elegance of his mind:
I knew a phoenix in my youth, so let them have their day.

The young men every night applaud their Gaby's laughing eye,
And Ruth St Denis had more charm although she had poor luck;
From nineteen hundred nine or ten, Pavlova's had the cry,
And there's a player in the States who gathers up her cloak
And flings herself out of the room when Juliet would be bride
With all a woman's passion, a child's imperious way,
And there are — but no matter if there are scores beside:
I knew a phoenix in my youth, so let them have their day.

There's Margaret and Marjorie and Dorothy and Nan,
A Daphne and a Mary who live in privacy;
One's had her fill of lovers, another's had but one,
Another boasts, 'I pick and choose and have but two or three.'
If head and limb have beauty and the instep's high and light
They can spread out what sail they please for all I have to say,
Be but the breakers of men's hearts or engines of delight:
I knew a phoenix in my youth, so let them have their day.

There'll be that crowd, that barbarous crowd, through all the centuries,
And who can say but some young belle may walk and talk men wild
Who is my beauty's equal, though that my heart denies,
But not the exact likeness, the simplicity of a child,
And that proud look as though she had gazed into the burning sun,
And all the shapely body no tittle gone astray.
I mourn for that most lonely thing; and yet God's will be done:
I knew a phoenix in my youth, so let them have their day.

A PRAYER ON GOING INTO MY HOUSE

God grant a blessing on this tower and cottage
And on my heirs, if all remain unspoiled,
No table or chair or stool not simple enough
For shepherd lads in Galilee; and grant
That I myself for portions of the year
May handle nothing and set eyes on nothing
But what the great and passionate have used
Throughout so many varying centuries
We take it for the norm; yet should I dream
Sinbad the sailor's brought a painted chest,
Or image, from beyond the Loadstone Mountain,
That dream is a norm; and should some limb of the Devil
Destroy the view by cutting down an ash
That shades the road, or setting up a cottage
Planned in a government office, shorten his life,
Manacle his soul upon the Red Sea bottom.

Robert Gregory's vision of the Tower at Ballylee.

I

On the grey rock of Cashel the mind's eye
Has called up the cold spirits that are born
When the old moon is vanished from the sky
And the new still hides her horn.

Under blank eyes and fingers never still
The particular is pounded till it is man.
When had I my own will?
O not since life began.

Constrained, arraigned, baffled, bent and unbent
By these wire-jointed jaws and limbs of wood,
Themselves obedient,
Knowing not evil and good;

Obedient to some hidden magical breath.
They do not even feel, so abstract are they,
So dead beyond our death,
Triumph that we obey.

II

On the grey rock of Cashel I suddenly saw
A Sphinx with woman breast and lion paw,
A Buddha, hand at rest,
Hand lifted up that blest;

And right between these two a girl at play
That, it may be, had danced her life away,
For now being dead it seemed
That she of dancing dreamed.

Although I saw it all in the mind's eye
There can be nothing solider till I die;
I saw by the moon's light
Now at its fifteenth night.

One lashed her tail; her eyes lit by the moon
Gazed upon all things known, all things unknown,
In triumph of intellect
With motionless head erect.

That other's moonlit eyeballs never moved,
Being fixed on all things loved, all things unloved,
Yet little peace he had,
For those that love are sad.

O little did they care who danced between,
And little she by whom her dance was seen
So she had outdanced thought.
Body perfection brought,

For what but eye and ear silence the mind
With the minute particulars of mankind?
Mind moved yet seemed to stop
As 'twere a spinning-top.

In contemplation had those three so wrought
Upon a moment, and so stretched it out
That they, time overthrown,
Were dead yet flesh and bone.

III

I knew that I had seen, had seen at last
That girl my unremembering nights hold fast
Or else my dreams that fly
If I should rub an eye,

And yet in flying fling into my meat
A crazy juice that makes the pulses beat
As though I had been undone
By Homer's Paragon

Who never gave the burning town a thought;
To such a pitch of folly I am brought,
Being caught between the pull
Of the dark moon and the full,

The commonness of thought and images
That have the frenzy of our western seas.
Thereon I made my moan,
And after kissed a stone,

And after that arranged it in a song
Seeing that I, ignorant for so long,
Had been rewarded thus
In Cormac's ruined house.

The Grey Rock of Cashel.

*As the popular (nationalistic) imagination
saw the birth of the Irish Republic in 1916.*

There is a paradox here, one of those 'wells that shine and are as shallow as pools'. The title-poem comes from that mystical world we have just mentioned, as do other poems in the gathering. The poems we print here such as 'Easter 1916' (p. 92) and 'Sixteen Dead Men' (p. 96) relate, mostly, to the harsh and brutal, and sad, realities of the revolutionary Ireland of that time.

The poet was not, needless to say, the only person to be taken by surprise by the armed revolution of 1916. It is quite possible that even some of those most fatally involved were swept onwards in a state of semi-comprehension. In such matters there are always beavers busy in the background. There had been so much fine talk from Westport, Mayo, to Westminster, England, about that not-far-distant day or date when the ship of Irish Home Rule would sail into port; there had been roaring talk about Ulster, as it was not quite accurately described, ready to resist in arms a Home Rule that might be Rome Rule: and then all Europe exploded, in the war that would create England's difficulty which would be Ireland's opportunity. That sentence had been so often repeated that the newsboys on the street could have whistled a tune to it.

But the wild talk and the windy talk of politicians, and the polite meaningless words spoken to young men on the streets, and the casual comedy of Dublin life, or any life, ended abruptly. And the poet was driven to consider men changed utterly by bewildered excess of love and by tragic death, ordinary men standing back into transfiguring Time to converse bone-to-bone with tragic figures of the past; and the ultimate of that one sad man who thought that for the salvation of a people there must be a blood-letting in every generation.

Well, it was the European fashion of that season. A young English poet, by the name of Brooke, was about then talking somewhat similar nonsense: about pouring out the red sweet wine of youth. The Battle of the Somme may have helped some sadder and wiser men to say Goodbye to All That.

For her participation in the 1916 Rising, Constance Markiewicz, the Irish wife of a Polish count who was much involved in the Dublin world of theatre, went to prison and was fortunate to escape a worse, and more immediate fate. She was, indeed, condemned to death. The legend of the grey gull that flew down to the barred window of her cell has become a rather lovely fragment of our patriotic martyrology, confirmed for ever by the poem 'On a Political Prisoner' (p. 94). Yeats remembers her as, in another majestic poem, he is to remember her sister, Eva, and herself, the Gore-Booth girls from the Great House of Lissadell by the Sligo sea; he recalls her when she was young and beautiful and merely impetuous, and riding to hounds on the middling level land under the awesome forehead of Ben Bulben.

Most appropriately, the visionary and prophetic poem that follows, 'The Second Coming' (p. 94), hails from a background of destruction and bloodshed and that growing murderousness of man, and of man's increasing ability to indulge his murderous instincts in the most scientific fashion. Has the Christian dispensation ended and what, out of the burning desert, is coming towards us to replace it? Shelley's Ozymandias, King of Kings, or what was left of him, could have stood, two vast and trunkless legs of stone, in that same desert.

But how, prophetic? Well, consider what the world, and even a small corner of this small island, has seen and endured since William Yeats died in 1939.

Yeats was to ask in another poem, 'But is there any comfort to be found?' And in 'A Prayer for My Daughter' (p. 98) he prays to whatever gods there be (as Swinburne, whom John Yeats loathed, might have put it) for some sign of permanence, for the preservation of ancient custom and ceremony.

In the tower of Ballylee he looks down on his infant daughter asleep in the cradle. The storm, bred on the Atlantic and roaring over Gregory's wood, could well be that world of destruction with all its murderousness. The prayer needs no comment. But in that troubled world he prays against hatred and the opinionated mind that can even deform beauty. Whatever gods there be should have been placated by such a prayer.

Then he makes his own personal gesture against Time, the transfigurer, in the six resounding lines to be carved on a stone at Thoor Ballylee (p. 99) and to remain with the restored and preserved tower. The tower still stands and the stone can be read.

I have met them at close of day
Coming with vivid faces
From counter or desk among grey
Eighteenth-century houses.
I have passed with a nod of the head
Or polite meaningless words,
Or have lingered awhile and said
Polite meaningless words,
And thought before I had done
Of a mocking tale or a gibe
To please a companion
Around the fire at the club,
Being certain that they and I
But lived where motley is worn:
All changed, changed utterly:
A terrible beauty is born.

That woman's days were spent
In ignorant good-will,
Her nights in argument
Until her voice grew shrill.
What voice more sweet than hers
When, young and beautiful,
She rode to harriers?
This man had kept a school
And rode our wingèd horse;
This other his helper and friend
Was coming into his force;
He might have won fame in the end,
So sensitive his nature seemed,
So daring and sweet his thought.
This other man I had dreamed
A drunken, vainglorious lout.
He had done most bitter wrong
To some who are near my heart,
Yet I number him in the song;
He, too, has resigned his part
In the casual comedy;
He, too, has been changed in his turn,
Transformed utterly:
A terrible beauty is born.

Hearts with one purpose alone
Through summer and winter seem
Enchanted to a stone
To trouble the living stream.

The horse that comes from the road,
The rider, the birds that range
From cloud to tumbling cloud,
Minute by minute they change;
A shadow of cloud on the stream
Changes minute by minute;
A horse-hoof slides on the brim,
And a horse plashes within it;
The long-legged moor-hens dive,
And hens to moor-cocks call;
Minute by minute they live:
The stone's in the midst of all.

Too long a sacrifice
Can make a stone of the heart.
O when may it suffice?
That is Heaven's part, our part
To murmur name upon name,
As a mother names her child
When sleep at last has come
On limbs that had run wild.
What is it but nightfall?
No, no, not night but death;
Was it needless death after all?
For England may keep faith
For all that is done and said.
We know their dream; enough
To know they dreamed and are dead;
And what if excess of love
Bewildered them till they died?
I write it out in a verse —
MacDonagh and MacBride
And Connolly and Pearse
Now and in time to be,
Wherever green is worn,
Are changed, changed utterly:
A terrible beauty is born.

September 25, 1916

The Post Office ... after the bombardment ... 1916.

ON A POLITICAL PRISONER

She that but little patience knew,
From childhood on, had now so much
A grey gull lost its fear and flew
Down to her cell and there alit,
And there endured her fingers' touch
And from her fingers ate its bit.

Did she in touching that lone wing
Recall the years before her mind
Became a bitter, an abstract thing,
Her thought some popular enmity:
Blind and leader of the blind
Drinking the foul ditch where they lie?

When long ago I saw her ride
Under Ben Bulben to the meet,
The beauty of her country-side
With all youth's lonely wildness stirred,
She seemed to have grown clean and sweet
Like any rock-bred, sea-borne bird:

Sea-borne, or balanced on the air
When first it sprang out of the nest
Upon some lofty rock to stare
Upon the cloudy canopy,
While under its storm-beaten breast
Cried out the hollows of the sea.

THE SECOND COMING

Turning and turning in the widening gyre
The falcon cannot hear the falconer;
Things fall apart; the centre cannot hold;
Mere anarchy is loosed upon the world,
The blood-dimmed tide is loosed, and everywhere
The ceremony of innocence is drowned;
The best lack all conviction, while the worst
Are full of passionate intensity.

Surely some revelation is at hand;
Surely the Second Coming is at hand.
The Second Coming! Hardly are those words out
When a vast image out of *Spiritus Mundi*
Troubles my sight: somewhere in sands of the desert
A shape with lion body and the head of a man,
A gaze blank and pitiless as the sun,
Is moving its slow thighs, while all about it
Reel shadows of the indignant desert birds.
The darkness drops again; but now I know
That twenty centuries of stony sleep
Were vexed to nightmare by a rocking cradle,
And what rough beast, its hour come round at last,
Slouches towards Bethlehem to be born?

The Countess Markiewicz (Constance Gore-Booth), seen through a cellar window of Liberty Hall, 1916.

COMMUNICATING WITH THE PRISONERS, 1924, *by Jack B. Yeats (Kilmainham Jail).*

O but we talked at large before
The sixteen men were shot,
But who can talk of give and take,
What should be and what not
While those dead men are loitering there
To stir the boiling pot?

You say that we should still the land
Till Germany's overcome;
But who is there to argue that
Now Pearse is deaf and dumb?
And is their logic to outweigh
MacDonagh's bony thumb?

How could you dream they'd listen
That have an ear alone
For those new comrades they have found,
Lord Edward and Wolfe Tone,
Or meddle with our give and take
That converse bone to bone?

THE ROSE TREE

'O words are lightly spoken,'
Said Pearse to Connolly,
'Maybe a breath of politic words
Has withered our Rose Tree;
Or maybe but a wind that blows
Across the bitter sea.'

'It needs to be but watered,'
James Connolly replied,
'To make the green come out again
And spread on every side,
And shake the blossom from the bud
To be the garden's pride.'

'But where can we draw water,'
Said Pearse to Connolly,
'When all the wells are parched away?
O plain as plain can be
There's nothing but our own red blood
Can make a right Rose Tree.'

Connolly's Irish Citizen Army, in full array, outside the old Liberty Hall, 1916.

Once more the storm is howling, and half hid
Under this cradle-hood and coverlid
My child sleeps on. There is no obstacle
But Gregory's wood and one bare hill
Whereby the haystack- and roof-levelling wind,
Bred on the Atlantic, can be stayed;
And for an hour I have walked and prayed
Because of the great gloom that is in my mind.

I have walked and prayed for this young child an hour
And heard the sea-wind scream upon the tower,
And under the arches of the bridge, and scream
In the elms above the flooded stream;
Imagining in excited reverie
That the future years had come,
Dancing to a frenzied drum,
Out of the murderous innocence of the sea.

May she be granted beauty and yet not
Beauty to make a stranger's eye distraught,
Or hers before a looking-glass, for such,
Being made beautiful overmuch,
Consider beauty a sufficient end,
Lose natural kindness and maybe
The heart-revealing intimacy
That chooses right, and never find a friend.

Helen being chosen found life flat and dull
And later had much trouble from a fool,
While that great Queen, that rose out of the spray,
Being fatherless could have her way
Yet chose a bandy-leggèd smith for man.
It's certain that fine women eat
A crazy salad with their meat
Whereby the Horn of Plenty is undone.

In courtesy I'd have her chiefly learned;
Hearts are not had as a gift but hearts are earned
By those that are not entirely beautiful;
Yet many, that have played the fool
For beauty's very self, has charm made wise,
And many a poor man that has roved,
Loved and thought himself beloved,
From a glad kindness cannot take his eyes.

May she become a flourishing hidden tree
That all her thoughts may like the linnet be,
And have no business but dispensing round
Their magnanimities of sound,
Nor but in merriment begin a chase,
Nor but in merriment a quarrel.
O may she live like some green laurel
Rooted in one dear perpetual place.

My mind, because the minds that I have loved,
The sort of beauty that I have approved,
Prosper but little, has dried up of late,
Yet knows that to be choked with hate
May well be of all evil chances chief.
If there's no hatred in a mind
Assault and battery of the wind
Can never tear the linnet from the leaf.

An intellectual hatred is the worst,
So let her think opinions are accursed.
Have I not seen the loveliest woman born
Out of the mouth of Plenty's horn,
Because of her opinionated mind
Barter that horn and every good
By quiet natures understood
For an old bellows full of angry wind?

Considering that, all hatred driven hence,
The soul recovers radical innocence
And learns at last that it is self-delighting,
Self-appeasing, self-affrighting,
And that its own sweet will is Heaven's will;
She can, though every face should scowl
And every windy quarter howl
Or every bellows burst, be happy still.

And may her bridegroom bring her to a house
Where all's accustomed, ceremonious;
For arrogance and hatred are the wares
Peddled in the thoroughfares.
How but in custom and in ceremony
Are innocence and beauty born?
Ceremony's a name for the rich horn,
And custom for the spreading laurel tree.

June 1919

TO BE CARVED ON A STONE
AT THOOR BALLYLEE

I, the poet William Yeats,
With old mill boards and sea-green slates,
And smithy work from the Gort forge,
Restored this tower for my wife George;
And may these characters remain
When all is ruin once again.

The front cover design for
The Tower, *1928,*
by T. Sturge Moore.

It seems to me, and will to many another, a sort of sacrilege and blasphemy combined to select from this 1928 gathering and to pass by the introductory poem, 'Sailing to Byzantium', one of the two tremendous offerings to Yeats' vision of ancient Byzantium and to an ordered society, as the poet saw and desired it. And not to worship for a while at the ancient altar to the legend of Leda in 'Leda and the Swan'.

But we maun, more or less, hold to our brief and hope only that no graven image will arise 'Of hammered gold and gold enamelling', to move and strike us down.

The tower of Ballylee is by now established as the poet's central and most notable symbol. Those old stone, square Norman and post-Norman towers are common enough in certain parts of Ireland.

And the poet continues quite reasonably or, perhaps, quite unreasonably to rage in 'The Tower' (p. 103) against Time and Old Age. He mentions Plato and Plotinus, and will again, to remind us in whose company we should walk if we wish to walk with him.

And in the second solemn movement of this transcendent poem he is again with Blind Raftery and Homer, and Mary Hynes, the Connacht rural beauty, and with the Lady Helen on the walls of Troy, and with the wraith of that other beauty who had so much tormented his earlier years; and with the thought, always gratifying to any poet, that the song could confer such glory on beauty that a man might, in the quest for it, go drunken crazy and drown in a marsh. And he walks again with Red Hanrahan, the bewitched poet astray in God-forsaken meadows.

With Mrs French and her shoneen and slave of a serving man, who mutilated the farmer, I have never, I confess, been quite happy, yet we may accept them as symbols from a simple time and a rude countryside. Ears, I feel, should be sacred. A nose, perhaps! But even then only after the severest provocation.

To the third movement of the poem one can but raise the hat and bow the knee.

Later he is to write the most striking epitaph ever composed for the Irish landed gentry and the passing of their way of life, and for the destruction and decay of their great houses before the land-wars and agitations of the second half of the nineteenth century, and for the changing economies of Europe and the Empire; and, finally, for the Jacquerie, in Ireland, of the violent 1920s.

In the opening stanzas of 'Meditations in Time of Civil War' (p. 107) he wonders, with Coole Park in mind, would Ireland and the world be any better off if such great houses should be no more? He considers then the home he had made in the tower and reflects on the tower as the symbol, through history, of the solitary, meditating mind. Later he will elaborate.

The changeless sword that lies on his table the poet sees as a portion of perfect art from a society ordered and unified as he had esteemed ancient Byzantium to be; as he, and some others, had desired Ireland to become. His attachment to the Japanese Noh plays begins in his imagining, and idealizing, such a society. For the sword was a gift to Yeats from a distinguished Japanese gentleman, Junzo Sato, when, in 1900, Yeats was on a lecture-tour in the USA.

Then he broods upon the future and on those who will come after him, but there is pride, and no uneasy foreboding, in the lines.

And he talks, at the door of the tower, to that 'affable Irregular', one of the patriots who would not accept the treaty, or truce, with England or with anyone else; and later he talks to the 'brown Lieutenant and his men' of the newly established army of the newly established Irish Free State. The 'cold snows of a dream' would seem to provide the proper climate for the brutal civil war that was then upon the roads of Ireland.

And he goes on to consider, in heart-rending lines, the plight of the heart grown brutal by feeding on fantasies that draw it away from the needs of human beings, and he pleads with the honey bees to come build in the hole the starlings have abandoned, and to bring their sweetness with them.

The seventh and final meditation brings us into an awesome world away beyond that in which we see and move.

In a dedicatory poem to his prose-fantasy, *The Napoleon of Notting Hill*, a poem with some wisdom, moments of revelation, and a certain shot of fatuity, G. K. Chesterton seemed prepared to welcome a revival, or intensification, of local patriotisms and the frictions between neighbours which such patriotisms might bring with them. In all that, he saw the overturning of some theories which were around at the end of the last century: that such nationalisms would pass and take wars with them. He lived to see that he was right but it is unlikely that he, or anybody else, enjoyed the realization.

Yeats, considering the appalling European war and the minor savagery in Ireland, more wisely meditated in 'Nineteen Hundred and Nineteen' (p. 110) on the way in which man could destroy man and the works of man: right down from the masterpieces of Phidias – the wonders, we are told, of the ancient world – to the killing of a woman in the town of Gort by drunken Black-and-Tans driving through and firing at random.

The weasels, or perhaps stoats, he heard on a roadside near Ballylee. They provided him with a fearful image of the, shall we say, least amiable aspects of human life; and the vision of the dragon of the air, which the Chinese dancers made out of radiant, floating silk scarves, comes almost as a happy relief, even if we are forced to accept the fatalistic conclusion that we dance, or live, whether we will or no, to a beat over which we have little or no control.

In the third movement of what is certainly one of the noblest of Yeats' poems, he is again with the magical swan but, in the mood of the time, the heaven towards which the great bird clamours is desolate.

Mankind rejoices obscenely in the display of the weasel's tooth. And it is time to mock at the great: 'Look on my works, ye mighty, and despair.' And to mock even at the wise and the good, and to mock at the mockers while the storm of the world beats on the window.

The brief and difficult prayer that follows (p. 112) is best explained by John Unterecker. It brings us again to the threshold of the Occult and to the automatic writing which George Yeats practised and which, her husband believed, evoked other-worldly influences. It looks back to 'The Second Coming' and forward to the completed version of *A Vision*. John Unterecker wrote:

But if there is any pattern in Yeats, it is that of life's ultimate triumph over death. And 'A Prayer For My Son' follows hard on those poems which explore the death-wish. Some of the minor problems of the poem can be disposed of if one recalls Yeats' note in 'A Packet For Ezra Pound', to the effect that he had been warned in the automatic writing that the 'Frustrators', who had made difficult the dictation of that script, were planning an attack on his health and the health of his children. The ghost he calls on at the beginning of the second stanza is therefore a kind of hearth-god who will guard young William Michael (born August 22, 1921) from the evil forces that oppose a poet's son.

In 1924, when Yeats was fifty-nine years of age, he wrote the wryly amusing quatrain 'Youth and Age':

Much did I rage when young,
Being by the world oppressed,
But now with flattering tongue
It speeds the parting guest.

Now a little later he can, with some justification, describe himself in 'Among School Children' (p. 114) as a 'sixty-year-old smiling public man'.

He is a Senator of the new Irish Free State. His admiring friend, Joseph O'Neill, is secretary of the Department of Education. Through O'Neill, and other influences within the Senate, the poet finds himself involved in the visiting (not inspection, as has been wrongly said) of some primary schools, and wondering whether any of us live up to any promise we may have given, and thinking of that Ledaean body, once also that of a schoolgirl, which had tormented many years of his life and is now bent, in accursed old age, above a sinking fire.

THE TOWER

I

What shall I do with this absurdity –
O heart, O troubled heart – this caricature,
Decrepit age that has been tied to me
As to a dog's tail?
                        Never had I more
Excited, passionate, fantastical
Imagination, nor an ear and eye
That more expected the impossible–
No, not in boyhood when with rod and fly,
Or the humbler worm, I climbed Ben Bulben's back
And had the livelong summer day to spend.
It seems that I must bid the Muse go pack
Choose Plato and Plotinus for a friend
Until imagination, ear and eye,
Can be content with argument and deal
In abstract things; or be derided by
A sort of battered kettle at the heel.

II

I pace upon the battlements and stare
On the foundations of a house, or where
Tree, like a sooty finger, starts from the earth;
And send imagination forth
Under the day's declining beam, and call
Images and memories
From ruin or from ancient trees,
For I would ask a question of them all.

Beyond that ridge lived Mrs French, and once
When every silver candlestick or sconce
Lit up the dark mahogany and the wine,
A serving-man, that could divine
That most respected lady's every wish,
Ran and with the garden shears
Clipped an insolent farmer's ears
And brought them in a little covered dish.

Some few remembered still when I was young
A peasant girl commended by a song,
Who'd lived somewhere upon that rocky place,
And praised the colour of her face,
And had the greater joy in praising her,
Remembering that, if walked she there,
Farmers jostled at the fair
So great a glory did the song confer.

And certain men, being maddened by those rhymes,
Or else by toasting her a score of times,
Rose from the table and declared it right
To test their fancy by their sight;
But they mistook the brightness of the moon
For the prosaic light of day –
Music had driven their wits astray –
And one was drowned in the great bog of Cloone.

Strange, but the man who made the song was blind;
Yet, now I have considered it, I find
That nothing strange; the tragedy began
With Homer that was a blind man,
And Helen has all living hearts betrayed.
O may the moon and sunlight seem
One inextricable beam,
For if I triumph I must make men mad.

And I myself created Hanrahan
And drove him drunk or sober through the dawn
From somewhere in the neighbouring cottages.
Caught by an old man's juggleries
He stumbled, tumbled, fumbled to and fro
And had but broken knees for hire
And horrible splendour of desire;
I thought it all out twenty years ago:

Good fellows shuffled cards in an old bawn;
And when that ancient ruffian's turn was on
He so bewitched the cards under his thumb
That all but the one card became
A pack of hounds and not a pack of cards,
And that he changed into a hare.
Hanrahan rose in frenzy there
And followed up those baying creatures towards—

O towards I have forgotten what—enough!
I must recall a man that neither love
Nor music nor an enemy's clipped ear
Could, he was so harried, cheer;
A figure that has grown so fabulous
There's not a neighbour left to say
When he finished his dog's day:
An ancient bankrupt master of this house.

Before that ruin came, for centuries,
Rough men-at-arms, cross-gartered to the knees
Or shod in iron, climbed the narrow stairs,
And certain men-at-arms there were
Whose images, in the Great Memory stored,
Come with loud cry and panting breast
To break upon a sleeper's rest
While their great wooden dice beat on the board.

As I would question all, come all who can;
Come old, necessitous, half-mounted man;
And bring beauty's blind rambling celebrant;
The red man the juggler sent
Through God-forsaken meadows; Mrs French,
Gifted with so fine an ear;
The man drowned in a bog's mire,
When mocking Muses chose the country wench.

Did all old men and women, rich and poor,
Who trod upon these rocks or passed this door,
Whether in public or in secret rage
As I do now against old age?
But I have found an answer in those eyes
That are impatient to be gone;
Go therefore; but leave Hanrahan,
For I need all his mighty memories.

Old lecher with a love on every wind,
Bring up out of that deep considering mind
All that you have discovered in the grave,
For it is certain that you have
Reckoned up every unforeknown, unseeing
Plunge, lured by a softening eye,
Or by a touch or a sigh,
Into the labyrinth of another's being;

Does the imagination dwell the most
Upon a woman won or woman lost?
If on the lost, admit you turned aside
From a great labyrinth out of pride,
Cowardice, some silly over-subtle thought
Or anything called conscience once;
And that if memory recur, the sun's
Under eclipse and the day blotted out.

III

It is time that I wrote my will;
I choose upstanding men
That climb the streams until
The fountain leap, and at dawn
Drop their cast at the side
Of dripping stone; I declare
They shall inherit my pride,
The pride of people that were
Bound neither to Cause nor to State,
Neither to slaves that were spat on,
Nor to the tyrants that spat,
The people of Burke and of Grattan
That gave, though free to refuse –
Pride, like that of the morn,
When the headlong light is loose,
Or that of the fabulous horn,
Or that of the sudden shower
When all streams are dry,
Or that of the hour
When the swan must fix his eye
Upon a fading gleam,
Float out upon a long
Last reach of glittering stream
And there sing his last song.
And I declare my faith:
I mock Plotinus' thought
And cry in Plato's teeth,
Death and life were not
Till man made up the whole,
Made lock, stock and barrel
Out of his bitter soul,
Aye, sun and moon and star, all,
And further add to that
That, being dead, we rise,
Dream and so create
Translunar Paradise.
I have prepared my peace
With learned Italian things
And the proud stones of Greece,
Poet's imaginings
And memories of love,
Memories of the words of women,
All those things whereof
Man makes a superhuman
Mirror-resembling dream.

As at the loophole there
The daws chatter and scream,
And drop twigs layer upon layer,
When they have mounted up,
The mother bird will rest
On their hollow top,
And so warm her wild nest.

I leave both faith and pride
To young upstanding men
Climbing the moutain-side,
That under bursting dawn
They may drop a fly;
Being of that metal made
Till it was broken by
This sedentary trade.

Now shall I make my soul,
Compelling it to study
In a learned school
Till the wreck of body,
Slow decay of blood,
Testy delirium
Or dull decrepitude,
Or what worse evil come –
The death of friends, or death
Of every brilliant eye
That made a catch in the breath –
Seem but the clouds of the sky
When the horizon fades;
Or a bird's sleepy cry
Among the deepening shades.

1926

I

Ancestral Houses

Surely among a rich man's flowering lawns,
Amid the rustle of his planted hills,
Life overflows without ambitious pains;
And rains down life until the basin spills,
And mounts more dizzy high the more it rains
As though to choose whatever shape it wills
And never stoop to a mechanical
Or servile shape, at others' beck and call.

Mere dreams, mere dreams! Yet Homer had not sung
Had he not found it certain beyond dreams
That out of life's own self-delight had sprung
The abounding glittering jet; though now it seems
As if some marvellous empty sea-shell flung
Out of the obscure dark of the rich streams,
And not a fountain, were the symbol which
Shadows the inherited glory of the rich.

Some violent bitter man, some powerful man
Called architect and artist in, that they,
Bitter and violent men, might rear in stone
The sweetness that all longed for night and day,
The gentleness none there had ever known;
But when the master's buried mice can play,
And maybe the great-grandson of that house,
For all its bronze and marble, 's but a mouse.

O what if gardens where the peacock strays
With delicate feet upon old terraces,
Or else all Juno from an urn displays
Before the indifferent garden deities;
O what if levelled lawns and gravelled ways
Where slippered Contemplation finds his ease
And Childhood a delight for every sense,
But take our greatness with our violence?

What if the glory of escutcheoned doors,
And buildings that a haughtier age designed,
The pacing to and fro on polished floors
Amid great chambers and long galleries, lined
With famous portraits of our ancestors;
What if those things the greatest of mankind
Consider most to magnify, or to bless,
But take our greatness with our bitterness?

THE MEN OF THE WEST.
The painter Seán Keating (1889–1978) cast his
mind, perhaps, on the Year of the French – 1798 –
when General Humbert landed.

II

My House

An ancient bridge, and a more ancient tower,
A farmhouse that is sheltered by its wall,
An acre of stony ground,
Where the symbolic rose can break in flower,
Old ragged elms, old thorns innumerable,
The sound of the rain or sound
Of every wind that blows;
The stilted water-hen
Crossing stream again
Scared by the splashing of a dozen cows;
A winding stair, a chamber arched with stone,
A grey stone fireplace with an open hearth,
A candle and written page.
Il Penseroso's Platonist toiled on
In some like chamber, shadowing forth
How the daemonic rage
Imagined everything.
Benighted travellers
From markets and from fairs
Have seen his midnight candle glimmering.

Two men have founded here. A man-at-arms
Gathered a score of horse and spent his days
In this tumultuous spot,
Where through long wars and sudden night alarms
His dwindling score and he seemed castaways
Forgetting and forgot;
And I, that after me
My bodily heirs may find,
To exalt a lonely mind,
Befitting emblems of adversity.

III

My Table

Two heavy trestles, and a board
Where Sato's gift, a changeless sword,
By pen and paper lies,
That it may moralise
My days out of their aimlessness.
A bit of an embroidered dress
Covers its wooden sheath.
Chaucer had not drawn breath
When it was forged. In Sato's house,
Curved like new moon, moon-luminous,
It lay five hundred years.
Yet if no change appears
No moon; only an aching heart
Conceives a changeless work of art.

Our learned men have urged
That when and where 'twas forged
A marvellous accomplishment,
In painting or in pottery, went
From father unto son
And through the centuries ran
And seemed unchanging like the sword.
Soul's beauty being most adored,
Men and their business took
The soul's unchanging look
For the most rich inheritor,
Knowing that none could pass Heaven's door
That loved inferior art,
Had such an aching heart
That he, although a country's talk
For silken clothes and stately walk,
Had waking wits; it seemed
Juno's peacock screamed.

IV

My Descendants

Having inherited a vigorous mind
From my old fathers, I must nourish dreams
And leave a woman and a man behind
As vigorous of mind, and yet it seems
Life scarce can cast a fragrance on the wind,
Scarce spread a glory to the morning beams,
But the torn petals strew the garden plot;
And there's but common greenness after that.

And what if my descendants lose the flower
Through natural declension of the soul,
Through too much business with the passing hour,
Through too much play, or marriage with a fool?
May this laborious stair and this stark tower
Become a roofless ruin that the owl
May build in the cracked masonry and cry
Her desolation to the desolate sky.

The Primum Mobile that fashioned us
Has made the very owls in circles move;
And I, that count myself most prosperous,
Seeing that love and friendship are enough,
For an old neighbour's friendship chose the house
And decked and altered it for a girl's love,
And know whatever flourish and decline
These stones remain their monument and mine.

V

The Road at My Door
An affable Irregular,
A heavily-built Falstaffian man,
Comes cracking jokes of civil war
As though to die by gunshot were
The finest play under the sun.

A brown Lieutenant and his men,
Half dressed in national uniform,
Stand at my door, and I complain
Of the foul weather, hail and rain,
A pear-tree broken by the storm.

I count those feathered balls of soot
The moor-hen guides upon the stream,
To silence the envy in my thought;
And turn towards my chamber, caught
In the cold snows of a dream.

VI

The Stare's Nest by My Window
The bees build in the crevices
Of loosening masonry, and there
The mother birds bring grubs and flies.
My wall is loosening; honey-bees,
Come build in the empty house of the stare.

We are closed in, and the key is turned
On our uncertainty; somewhere
A man is killed, or a house burned,
Yet no clear fact to be discerned:
Come build in the empty house of the stare.

A barricade of stone or of wood;
Some fourteen days of civil war;
Last night they trundled down the road
That dead young soldier in his blood:
Come build in the empty house of the stare.

We had fed the heart on fantasies,
The heart's grown brutal from the fare;
More substance in our enmities
Than in our love; O honey-bees,
Come build in the empty house of the stare.

VII

I see Phantoms of Hatred and of the Heart's Fullness
and of the Coming Emptiness
I climb to the tower-top and lean upon broken stone,
A mist that is like blown snow is sweeping over all,
Valley, river, and elms, under the light of a moon
That seems unlike itself, that seems unchangeable,
A glittering sword out of the east. A puff of wind
And those white glimmering fragments of the mist sweep by.
Frenzies bewilder, reveries perturb the mind;
Monstrous familiar images swim to the mind's eye.

'Vengeance upon the murderers,' the cry goes up,
'Vengeance for Jacques Molay.' In cloud-pale rags, or in lace,
The rage-driven, rage-tormented, and rage-hungry troop,
Trooper belabouring trooper, biting at arm or at face,
Plunges towards nothing, arms and fingers spreading wide
For the embrace of nothing; and I, my wits astray
Because of all that senseless tumult, all but cried
For vengeance on the murderers of Jacques Molay.

Their legs long, delicate and slender, aquamarine their eyes,
Magical unicorns bear ladies on their backs.
The ladies close their musing eyes. No prophecies,
Remembered out of Babylonian almanacs,
Have closed the ladies' eyes, their minds are but a pool
Where even longing drowns under its own excess;
Nothing but stillness can remain when hearts are full
Of their own sweetness, bodies of their loveliness.

The cloud-pale unicorns, the eyes of aquamarine,
The quivering half-closed eyelids, the rags of cloud or of lace,
Or eyes that rage has brightened, arms it has made lean,
Give place to an indifferent multitude, give place
To brazen hawks. Nor self-delighting reverie,
Nor hate of what's to come, nor pity for what's gone,
Nothing but grip of claw, and the eye's complacency,
The innumerable clanging wings that have put out the moon.

I turn away and shut the door, and on the stair
Wonder how many times I could have proved my worth
In something that all others understand or share;
But O! ambitious heart, had such a proof drawn forth
A company of friends, a conscience set at ease,
It had but made us pine the more. The abstract joy,
The half-read wisdom of daemonic images,
Suffice the ageing man as once the growing boy.

1923

I

Many ingenious lovely things are gone
That seemed sheer miracle to the multitude,
Protected from the circle of the moon
That pitches common things about. There stood
Amid the ornamental bronze and stone
An ancient image made of olive wood –
And gone are Phidias' famous ivories
And all the golden grasshoppers and bees.

We too had many pretty toys when young:
A law indifferent to blame or praise,
To bribe or threat; habits that made old wrong
Melt down, as it were wax in the sun's rays;
Public opinion ripening for so long
We thought it would outlive all future days.
O what fine thought we had because we thought
That the worst rogues and rascals had died out.

All teeth were drawn, all ancient tricks unlearned,
And a great army but a showy thing;
What matter that no cannon had been turned
Into a ploughshare? Parliament and king
Thought that unless a little powder burned
The trumpeters might burst with trumpeting
And yet it lack all glory; and perchance
The guardsmen's drowsy chargers would not prance.

Now days are dragon-ridden, the nightmare
Rides upon sleep: a drunken soldiery
Can leave the mother, murdered at her door,
To crawl in her own blood, and go scot-free;
The night can sweat with terror as before
We pieced our thoughts into philosophy,
And planned to bring the world under a rule,
Who are but weasels fighting in a hole.

He who can read the signs nor sink unmanned
Into the half-deceit of some intoxicant
From shallow wits; who knows no work can stand,
Whether health, wealth or peace of mind were spent
On master-work of intellect or hand,
No honour leave its mighty monument,
Has but one comfort left: all triumph would
But break upon his ghostly solitude.

But is there any comfort to be found?
Man is in love and loves what vanishes,
What more is there to say? That country round
None dared admit, if such a thought were his,
Incendiary or bigot could be found
To burn that stump on the Acropolis,
Or break in bits the famous ivories
Or traffic in the grasshoppers or bees.

II

When Loie Fuller's Chinese dancers enwound
A shining web, a floating ribbon of cloth,
It seemed that a dragon of air
Had fallen among dancers, had whirled them round
Or hurried them off on its own furious path;
So the Platonic Year
Whirls out new right and wrong,
Whirls in the old instead;
All men are dancers and their tread
Goes to the barbarous clangour of a gong.

III

Some moralist or mythological poet
Compares the solitary soul to a swan;
I am satisfied with that,
Satisfied if a troubled mirror show it,
Before that brief gleam of its life be gone,
An image of its state;
The wings half spread for flight,
The breast thrust out in pride
Whether to play, or to ride
Those winds that clamour of approaching night.

A man in his own secret meditation
Is lost amid the labyrinth that he has made
In art or politics;
Some Platonist affirms that in the station
Where we should cast off body and trade
The ancient habit sticks,
And that if our works could
But vanish with our breath
That were a lucky death,
For triumph can but mar our solitude.

The swan has leaped into the desolate heaven:
That image can bring wildness, bring a rage
To end all things, to end
What my laborious life imagined, even
The half-imagined, the half-written page;
O but we dreamed to mend
Whatever mischief seemed
To afflict mankind, but now
That winds of winter blow
Learn that we were crack-pated when we dreamed.

IV

We, who seven years ago
Talked of honour and of truth,
Shriek with pleasure if we show
The weasel's twist, the weasel's tooth.

V

Come let us mock at the great
That had such burdens on the mind
And toiled so hard and late
To leave some monument behind,
Nor thought of the levelling wind.

Come let us mock at the wise;
With all those calendars whereon
They fixed old aching eyes,
They never saw how seasons run,
And now but gape at the sun.

Come let us mock at the good
That fancied goodness might be gay,
And sick of solitude
Might proclaim a holiday:
Wind shrieked — and where are they?

Mock mockers after that
That would not lift a hand maybe
To help good, wise or great
To bar that foul storm out, for we
Traffic in mockery.

VI

Violence upon the roads: violence of horses;
Some few have handsome riders, are garlanded
On delicate sensitive ear or tossing mane,
But wearied running round and round in their courses
All break and vanish, and evil gathers head:
Herodias' daughters have returned again,
A sudden blast of dusty wind and after
Thunder of feet, tumult of images,
Their purpose in the labyrinth of the wind;
And should some crazy hand dare touch a daughter
All turn with amorous cries, or angry cries,
According to the wind, for all are blind.
But now wind drops, dust settles; thereupon
There lurches past, his great eyes without thought
Under the shadow of stupid straw-pale locks,
That insolent fiend Robert Artisson
To whom the love-lorn Lady Kyteler brought
Bronzed peacock feathers, red combs of her cocks.

1919

The Tans, posed and ready for action, on a Tipperary road.

Bid a strong ghost stand at the head
That my Michael may sleep sound,
Nor cry, nor turn in the bed
Till his morning meal come round;
And may departing twilight keep
All dread afar till morning's back,
That his mother may not lack
Her fill of sleep.

Bid the ghost have sword in fist:
Some there are, for I avow
Such devilish things exist,
Who have planned his murder, for they know
Of some most haughty deed or thought
That waits upon his future days,
And would through hatred of the bays
Bring that to nought.

Though You can fashion everything
From nothing every day, and teach
The morning stars to sing,
You have lacked articulate speech
To tell Your simplest want, and known,
Wailing upon a woman's knee,
All of that worst ignominy
Of flesh and bone;

And when through all the town there ran
The servants of Your enemy,
A woman and a man,
Unless the Holy Writings lie,
Hurried through the smooth and rough
And through the fertile and waste,
Protecting, till the danger past,
With human love.

Anne and Michael Yeats.

I

I walk through the long schoolroom questioning;
A kind old nun in a white hood replies;
The children learn to cipher and to sing,
To study reading-books and histories,
To cut and sew, be neat in everything
In the best modern way — the children's eyes
In momentary wonder stare upon
A sixty-year-old smiling public man.

II

I dream of a Ledaean body, bent
Above a sinking fire, a tale that she
Told of a harsh reproof, or trivial event
That changed some childish day to tragedy —
Told, and it seemed that our two natures blent
Into a sphere from youthful sympathy,
Or else, to alter Plato's parable,
Into the yolk and white of the one shell.

III

And thinking of that fit of grief or rage
I look upon one child or t'other there
And wonder if she stood so at that age —
For even daughters of the swan can share
Something of every paddler's heritage —
And had that colour upon cheek or hair,
And thereupon my heart is driven wild:
She stands before me as a living child.

IV

Her present image floats into the mind —
Did Quattrocento finger fashion it
Hollow of cheek as though it drank the wind
And took a mess of shadows for its meat?
And I though never of Ledaean kind
Had pretty plumage once — enough of that,
Better to smile on all that smile, and show
There is a comfortable kind of old scarecrow.

V

What youthful mother, a shape upon her lap
Honey of generation had betrayed,
And that must sleep, shriek, struggle to escape
As recollection or the drug decide,
Would think her son, did she but see that shape
With sixty or more winters on its head,
A compensation for the pang of his birth,
Or the uncertainty of his setting forth?

VI

Plato thought nature but a spume that plays
Upon a ghostly paradigm of things;
Solider Aristotle played the taws
Upon the bottom of a king of kings;
World-famous golden-thighed Pythagoras
Fingered upon a fiddle-stick or strings
What a star sang and careless Muses heard:
Old clothes upon old sticks to scare a bird.

VII

Both nuns and mothers worship images,
But those the candles light are not as those
That animate a mother's reveries,
But keep a marble or a bronze repose.
And yet they too break hearts — O Presences
That passion, piety or affection knows,
And that all heavenly glory symbolise —
O self-born mockers of man's enterprise;

VIII

Labour is blossoming or dancing where
The body is not bruised to pleasure soul,
Nor beauty born out of its own despair,
Nor blear-eyed wisdom out of midnight oil.
O chestnut-tree, great-rooted blossomer,
Are you the leaf, the blossom or the bole?
O body swayed to music, O brightening glance,
How can we know the dancer from the dance?

'All day in the one chair
From dream to dream and rhyme to rhyme I have ranged
In rambling talk with an image of air:
Vague memories, nothing but memories.'
'Broken Dreams'

W.B. Yeats as Seán O'Sullivan saw him in 1934.
The portrait is in the Abbey Theatre Collection.

THE WINDING STAIR AND
OTHER POEMS 1933

TO EDMUND DULAC

When he was twenty-nine years of age the poet wrote to his sister, Lily, that he had been staying at Lissadell House for a few days and had found the people of that Great House – one of the first places of that style he had known and which stayed in his mind as 'an image of aristocratic elegance' – to be delightful. He meant, above all, the two sisters, Constance and Eva Gore-Booth. Of Eva, who is still remembered by a few simple poems, he wrote, 'Miss Eva Gore-Booth shows some promise as a writer of verse. Her work is very formless as yet but it is full of telling little phrases.'

And of the house, 'Lissadell is an exceedingly impressive house inside with a great sitting-room high as a Church and all things in good taste . . .'

Constance was a more dramatic character than her sister and her life involved much tumult, in her marriage to the Polish count, Casimir Markiewicz, and in her intervention in politics and armed revolution.

In the poem 'In Memory of Eva Gore-Booth and Con Markiewicz' (p. 118) Yeats considers sadly what the years can do to the innocent and beautiful, and looks back at his own lost youth; and writes, as we have seen, the greatest epitaph or, perhaps, threnody for the passing of the Irish landed gentry.

Yeats once said that, according to what he had learned from MacGregor Mathers, his friend of the high and hazy, and mystical, days of the Hermetic Students of the Golden Dawn, that Solar meant all that was elaborate, full of artifice, whereas Water meant Lunar, and all that was simple, popular, traditional, emotional.

That circling moon, and the pitching of common things about, had ruled and overseen – rudely enough – seven centuries of Irish history, since the arrival of the Normans: what we used to take a masochistic kick from describing as the seven centuries of oppression.

The tower, and the winding stair that ascends within it, in 'Blood and the Moon' (p. 119), to the battlemented top, half-dead, and by that half-death mocking the present, stands for that history.

The great second movement of the poem traces that symbol of the tower back, by way of Shelley and the Pharos of Alexandria, to the ways of ancient Babylon, where, in one of his most memorable poems, A. E., from Portadown or Lurgan, as the case may be, had walked melodiously when the blue dusk ran between the streets and his love was winged within his mind.

But back to business, and the great statement in this poem expresses, most resonantly, the increasing devotion of Yeats to the aristocratic aspect, or ideal, of the Irish eighteenth century, as he saw it, and to its most memorable names: Goldsmith, Berkeley, Burke, Swift. They had, before him, trod that winding stair of history. He had come to think that their minds, combined with the ancient folk-wisdom, represented the best that Ireland could hope for or build on. Nobody, as far as I know, has yet said anything better to the contrary.

Meanwhile, the Great House of Lady Gregory at Coole, in which the poet had found so much composure and content, was nearing its end. In 1927 Lady Gregory had, by her own circumstances and those of the time, been forced to sell the house and the land to the Forestry Department. She stayed on as tenant. Some knowledge of the ecomonic and agrarian history of the country and of the great houses of the gentry may offer a reasonable explanation.

Yet it does seem a shame that the melancholy prophecy in the final verse of 'Coole Park, 1929' (p. 120) should have been fulfilled, and that nettles should have been seen to wave on the shapeless mound and saplings to root among the broken stone. The site, at least, has by now been made more acceptable and presentable. But men are we and must weep: and, also, for the passing of Frenchpark, the family home of Douglas Hyde, which, or so it seems to me, was even more sadly sacrificed.

So Yeats recalls Douglas Hyde and John Synge, and Shawe-Taylor and Hugh Lane, both nephews of the estimable Augusta Gregory, and sees himself a shy young man, ruffled in a manly pose, and goes on to consider the poet as the swan drifting on the darkening flood, in an altered and threatening world.

In St Patrick's Cathedral, in the heart of Old Dublin, you may read in the hallowed half-light Jonathan Swift's epitaph, cut in exact Latin. With a slight prefix Yeats gives it to us here in English (p. 123).

There was a fine suggestion once made that the poet Yeats, when he had sailed into his rest, should lie in Patrick's with the man he, rightly, so much admired.

In the end the poet elected to lie in the clay of Sligo, 'Under bare Ben Bulben's head'.

IN MEMORY OF EVA GORE-BOOTH AND CON MARKIEWICZ

The light of evening, Lissadell,
Great windows open to the south,
Two girls in silk kimonos, both
Beautiful, one a gazelle.
But a raving autumn shears
Blossom from the summer's wreath;
The older is condemned to death,
Pardoned, drags out lonely years
Conspiring among the ignorant.
I know not what the younger dreams —
Some vague Utopia — and she seems,
When withered old and skeleton-gaunt,
An image of such politics.
Many a time I think to seek
One or the other out and speak
Of that old Georgian mansion, mix
Pictures of the mind, recall
That table and the talk of youth,
Two girls in silk kimonos, both
Beautiful, one a gazelle.

Dear shadows, now you know it all,
All the folly of a fight
With a common wrong or right.
The innocent and the beautiful
Have no enemy but time;
Arise and bid me strike a match
And strike another till time catch;
Should the conflagration climb,
Run till all the sages know.
We the great gazebo built,
They convicted us of guilt;
Bid me strike a match and blow.

October 1927

*The Countess (Constance Gore-Booth),
painted by her husband, Casimir Markiewicz.*

I

Blessed be this place,
More blessed still this tower;
A bloody, arrogant power
Rose out of the race
Uttering, mastering it,
Rose like these walls from these
Storm/beaten cottages –
In mockery I have set
A powerful emblem up,
And sing it rhyme upon rhyme
In mockery of a time
Half dead at the top.

II

Alexandria's was a beacon tower, and Babylon's
An image of the moving heavens, a log/book of the sun's journey and the moon's;
And Shelley had his towers, thought's crowned powers he called them once.

I declare this tower is my symbol; I declare
This winding, gyring, spiring treadmill of a stair is my ancestral stair;
That Goldsmith and the Dean, Berkeley and Burke have travelled there.

Swift beating on his breast in sibylline frenzy blind
Because the heart in his blood/sodden breast had dragged him down into mankind,
Goldsmith deliberately sipping at the honey/pot of his mind,

And haughtier/headed Burke that proved the State a tree,
That this unconquerable labyrinth of the birds, century after century,
Cast but dead leaves to mathematical equality;

And God/appointed Berkeley that proved all things a dream,
That this pragmatical, preposterous pig of a world, its farrow that so solid seem,
Must vanish on the instant if the mind but change its theme;

Saeva Indignatio and the labourer's hire,
The strength that gives our blood and state magnanimity of its own desire;
Everything that is not God consumed with intellectual fire.

III
The purity of the unclouded moon
Has flung its arrowy shaft upon the floor.
Seven centuries have passed and it is pure,
The blood of innocence has left no stain.
There, on blood/saturated ground, have stood
Soldier, assassin, executioner,
Whether for daily pittance or in blind fear
Or out of abstract hatred, and shed blood,
But could not cast a single jet thereon.
Odour of blood on the ancestral stair!
And we that have shed none must gather there
And clamour in drunken frenzy for the moon.

IV
Upon the dusty, glittering windows cling,
And seem to cling upon the moonlit skies,
Tortoiseshell butterflies, peacock butterflies,
A couple of night/moths are on the wing.
Is every modern nation like the tower,
Half dead at the top? No matter what I said,
For wisdom is the property of the dead,
A something incompatible with life; and power,
Like everything that has the stain of blood,
A property of the living; but no stain
Can come upon the visage of the moon
When it has looked in glory from a cloud.

COOLE PARK, 1929

I meditate upon a swallow's flight,
Upon an aged woman and her house,
A sycamore and lime-tree lost in night
Although that western cloud is luminous,
Great works constructed there in nature's spite
For scholars and for poets after us,
Thoughts long knitted into a single thought,
A dance-like glory that those walls begot.

There Hyde before he had beaten into prose
That noble blade the Muses buckled on,
There one that ruffled in a manly pose
For all his timid heart, there that slow man,
That meditative man, John Synge, and those
Impetuous men, Shawe-Taylor and Hugh Lane,
Found pride established in humility,
A scene well set and excellent company.

They came like swallows and like swallows went,
And yet a woman's powerful character
Could keep a swallow to its first intent;
And half a dozen in formation there,
That seemed to whirl upon a compass-point,
Found certainty upon the dreaming air,
The intellectual sweetness of those lines
That cut through time or cross it withershins.

Here, traveller, scholar, poet, take your stand
When all those rooms and passages are gone,
When nettles wave upon a shapeless mound
And saplings root among the broken stone,
And dedicate – eyes bent upon the ground,
Back turned upon the brightness of the sun
And all the sensuality of the shade –
A moment's memory to that laurelled head.

(Left) Lady Gregory under the catalpa tree at
Coole Park, 1927.

(Right) Anglers on the lake at Coole: George
Russell, W.B. Yeats (left) and John Synge
(behind).

121

SWIFT'S EPITAPH

Swift has sailed into his rest;
Savage indignation there
Cannot lacerate his breast.
Imitate him if you dare,
World-besotted traveller; he
Served human liberty.

REMORSE FOR INTEMPERATE SPEECH

I ranted to the knave and fool,
But outgrew that school,
Would transform the part,
Fit audience found, but cannot rule
My fanatic* heart.

I sought my betters: though in each
Fine manners, liberal speech,
Turn hatred into sport,
Nothing said or done can reach
My fanatic heart.

Out of Ireland have we come.
Great hatred, little room,
Maimed us at the start.
I carry from my mother's womb
A fanatic heart.

August 28, 1931
*I pronounce 'fanatic' in what is,
I suppose, the older and more Irish way,
so that the last line of each stanza
contains but two beats.

*The heart of old Dublin, Patrick Street, and
St Patrick's – Swift's cathedral, painted in 1887
by Walter Osborne (1859–1903).*

COOLE PARK AND BALLYLEE, 1931

Under my window-ledge the waters race,
Otters below and moor-hens on the top,
Run for a mile undimmed in Heaven's face
Then darkening through 'dark' Raftery's 'cellar' drop,
Run underground, rise in a rocky place
In Coole demesne, and there to finish up
Spread to a lake and drop into a hole.
What's water but the generated soul?

Upon the border of that lake's a wood
Now all dry sticks under a wintry sun,
And in a copse of beeches there I stood,
For Nature's pulled her tragic buskin on
And all the rant's a mirror of my mood:
At sudden thunder of the mounting swan
I turned about and looked where branches break
The glittering reaches of the flooded lake.

Another emblem there! That stormy white
But seems a concentration of the sky;
And, like the soul, it sails into the sight
And in the morning's gone, no man knows why;
And is so lovely that it sets to right
What knowledge or its lack had set awry,
So arrogantly pure, a child might think
It can be murdered with a spot of ink.

Sound of a stick upon the floor, a sound
From somebody that toils from chair to chair;
Beloved books that famous hands have bound,
Old marble heads, old pictures everywhere;
Great rooms where travelled men and children found
Content or joy; a last inheritor
Where none has reigned that lacked a name and fame
Or out of folly into folly came.

A spot whereon the founders lived and died
Seemed once more dear than life; ancestral trees,
Or gardens rich in memory glorified
Marriages, alliances and families
And every bride's ambition satisfied.
Where fashion or mere fantasy decrees
We shift about—all that great glory spent—
Like some poor Arab tribesman and his tent.

We were the last romantics—chose for theme
Traditional sanctity and loveliness;
Whatever's written in what poets name
The book of the people; whatever most can bless
The mind of man or elevate a rhyme;
But all is changed, that high horse riderless,
Though mounted in that saddle Homer rode
Where the swan drifts upon a darkening flood.

We avail ourselves, here and now, of the winged liberty of the swan and leap into the heavens, in this case by no means desolate, and fly over the poet's lines written of St Kevin's, Glendalough, and over most of the Crazy Jane poems, and also that series of poems that reveals 'not just this woman's experience' but 'the experience of all women and all men', and over that sombre, complicated poem 'Parnell's Funeral', as well as much more.

We come, then, to 'Beautiful Lofty Things' (p. 126), Yeats' resonant celebration of the Olympians – surely not all, for only five are mentioned: his father, O'Leary the Fenian, Standish O'Grady who, with his *Bardic History of Ireland* has a fair claim to be among the father-founders of the Irish literary renaissance, and Augusta Gregory and Maud Gonne.

In the 1930s Dr Maloney wrote his book arguing that Sir Roger Casement's alleged diaries had been forged to blacken a good man's name in the eyes of such folk as disapproved of homosexuality, then a popular form of public disapproval, as instanced in the tragedy of Oscar Wilde. The theory was that such disapproval might take away from Casement the support of notable people who might otherwise intervene to save him from the scaffold on the charge of high treason and bringing in the Germans.

Yeats, who admired Casement for the nobility of his previous public and humanitarian career, was much moved by Dr Maloney's book.

He telephoned the literary editor of a Dublin newspaper to ask him, most modestly, would he accept some lines on the matter? This is of some personal interest to me because, as a literary editor, I succeeded that man, M. J. MacManus, a dear friend, who was always delighted to retell the story of how Mr Yeats came on the phone.

'Roger Casement' (p. 127) was initially printed in that newspaper and a controversy began that has not yet settled down. The poem was afterwards altered to, among other things, exclude the name of Alfred Noyes, who was able, sharply, to prove that he had not hand, act or any part in the dirty business.

Whatever the masters of the Empire hanged Casement for, it was not homosexuality. Even then, as H. G. Wells might have put it, etiquette was calmer. But in any crisis a Great Power may demand a scapegoat or two to prove to God, perhaps, and the world, that the Great Power is not guilty. The best the Empire could get after the Hitler war was a pathetic fellow by the name of Joyce.

The figure of Roger Casement still stands high above such sordidness: a most gallant gentleman.

The O'Rahilly (p. 128), Chief of the Clan O'Rahilly – as far as you or I or anybody else knows – was shot dead in a lane off Henry Street, Dublin City, in the fighting of 1916. An appealing, quixotic figure, he had stepped in half-innocent to find out that a rebellion was going on. Since he considered that some of his words and actions might have contributed to it, he stood honourably by to see the end of the affair: a gesture that would have fitted well into one of the poet's plays on the heroic ages.

The following trumpet-call, 'Come Gather Round Me, Parnellites' (p. 128) sounded so as to be heard into eternity by all who reverence the honour and memory of Charles Stewart Parnell, is, I am happy to say, occasionally to be heard recited above the glass in some places of Dublin public worship.

William Carleton, 1794–1869, had written that odd and comic story or fragment of autobiography *The Lough Derg Pilgrim*, describing how he, as a gormless young fellow with pious aspirations, had gone to the holy island on that northern lake where our patron saint and many others had been before him: an island sanctified, to the young William Yeats, by the verse of Calderón and the feet of centuries of pilgrims.

Many Irish writers have given thought to that holy place: Seán Ó Faoláin, Denis Devlin, Shane Leslie, Patrick Kavanagh and others, and, most recently, Séamus Heaney in his book *Station Island*.

In 'The Pilgrim' (p. 129) it would seem to me that

the ageing William Yeats may have been remembering, and echoing, William Carleton, for whom he had a high respect and in whose memory he spoke many fine words.

It was, as far as I remember, the subsequent poem, 'The Municipal Gallery Revisited' (p. 130), that set Frank O'Connor arguing that Yeats was, above all, the poet of friendship.

Most of the names mentioned in the poem are already familiar to us. But the portraits on the wall introduce two others: Arthur Griffith, the founder of Sinn Féin, a rational, self-dependent policy not to be confused with some contemporary gentlemen who, for reasons best known to themselves, continue to misuse the name. Griffith was, at times, opposed to Yeats in that whole, sad business of nationalism, but at least on one occasion was much in his favour.

Then there was Kevin O'Higgins, an iron-willed statesman, abominably murdered in the aftermath of the vile civil war.

And God be thanked, and on a happier note, there is Lady Lavery, the beautiful wife of the famous portrait-painter, Sir John Lavery.

The last verse of this poem has to be read over and over again, and out loud.

In the ballad that follows, 'John Kinsella's Lament for Mrs Mary Moore' (p. 132), more melancholy than randy, Yeats is back again with the folklore of rural places, but the mood and the style have much altered since the days of Yeats' early poetry. Well many things, since those days, have happened to Ireland and the poet.

On the quay of the harbour in Sligo town there was an old man who used to climb up on an abandoned, rusty boiler and rail against the world. See the poet's prose piece: *On the Boiler*. In 'Why Should Not Old Men Be Mad?' (p. 132) the ageing poet, considering this and that, feels entitled to wear the mask of that old man.

To write a great poem about the poet's own inability, or failing ability, to write any more poems is a staggering achievement. For the poet to see himself in 'The Circus Animals' Desertion' (p. 134) as a circus-ringmaster, and his themes as performing animals, displays an earth-shaking humour.

This must certainly be one of the most interesting examples of stock-taking in the long history of poetry.

The road from Sligo town to Bundoran, and beyond Bundoran into the wild beauty of County Donegal, is, in its early stages, dominated by a mountain notable in our ancient mythology.

In the Fenian saga *An Fhiannuidheacht*, the tales of Fionn MacCumhaill and his martial followers, the tale of the pursuit of Diarmuid and Gráinne – the golden, the beautiful – ends on that mountain in the death of Diarmuid, slain by his taboo animal, a wild boar.

Fionn, whose woman Diarmuid had stolen (or perhaps the strong-willed woman may have stolen Diarmuid) could have saved the life of Diarmuid with cupped hands filled with life-giving water, but Fionn malingered, and opened his hands: and Diarmuid died.

Appropriately enough, that mountain seems to follow you and to change shape as you go on, by the Sligo sea, towards Donegal. But it is certainly at its most impressive at Drumcliff churchyard where, by his command, the poet lies buried.

His last will and testament to the poets of Ireland, written down in 'Under Ben Bulben' (p. 136), ends with the words that are cut on his gravestone.

The poet, F. R. Higgins, told how he visited Yeats at his home at Rathfarnham, Dublin, on the night before Yeats left Ireland for the last time. He was to die in France.

Higgins remembered, 'After midnight we parted on the drive from his house. The head of the retiring figure, erect and challenging, gleamed through the darkness as I looked back; while, on the road before me, my thoughts were still singing with the slow, powerful accents of his chanting: "Irish poets, learn your trade ..."'

BEAUTIFUL LOFTY THINGS

Beautiful lofty things: O'Leary's noble head;
My father upon the Abbey stage, before him a raging crowd:
'This Land of Saints,' and then as the applause died out,
'Of plaster Saints'; his beautiful mischievous head thrown back.
Standish O'Grady supporting himself between the tables
Speaking to a drunken audience high nonsensical words;
Augusta Gregory seated at her great ormolu table,
Her eightieth winter approaching: 'Yesterday he threatened my life.
I told him that nightly from six to seven I sat at this table,
The blinds drawn up'; Maud Gonne at Howth station waiting a train,
Pallas Athene in that straight back and arrogant head:
All the Olympians; a thing never known again.

ROGER CASEMENT

(After reading 'The Forged Casement Diaries' by Dr Maloney)

I say that Roger Casement
Did what he had to do.
He died upon the gallows,
But that is nothing new.

Afraid they might be beaten
Before the bench of Time,
They turned a trick by forgery
And blackened his good name.

A perjurer stood ready
To prove their forgery true;
They gave it out to all the world,
And that is something new;

For Spring Rice had to whisper it,
Being their Ambassador,
And then the speakers got it
And writers by the score.

Come Tom and Dick, come all the troop
That cried it far and wide,
Come from the forger and his desk,
Desert the perjurer's side;

Come speak your bit in public
That some amends be made
To this most gallant gentleman
That is in quicklime laid.

THE GHOST OF ROGER CASEMENT

O what has made that sudden noise?
What on the threshold stands?
It never crossed the sea because
John Bull and the sea are friends;
But this is not the old sea
Nor this the old seashore.
What gave that roar of mockery,
That roar in the sea's roar?
The ghost of Roger Casement
Is beating on the door.

John Bull has stood for Parliament,
A dog must have his day,
The country thinks no end of him,
For he knows how to say,
At a beanfeast or a banquet,
That all must hang their trust
Upon the British Empire,
Upon the Church of Christ.
The ghost of Roger Casement
Is beating on the door.

John Bull has gone to India
And all must pay him heed,
For histories are there to prove
That none of another breed
Has had a like inheritance,
Or sucked such milk as he,
And there's no luck about a house
If it lack honesty.
The ghost of Roger Casement
Is beating on the door.

I poked about a village church
And found his family tomb
And copied out what I could read
In that religious gloom;
Found many a famous man there;
But fame and virtue rot.
Draw round, beloved and bitter men,
Draw round and raise a shout;
The ghost of Roger Casement
Is beating on the door.

Self-portrait (detail) by John Butler Yeats, 1907.

Sing of the O'Rahilly,
Do not deny his right;
Sing a 'the' before his name;
Allow that he, despite
All those learned historians,
Established it for good;
He wrote out that word himself,
He christened himself with blood.
                    How goes the weather?

Sing of the O'Rahilly
That had such little sense
He told Pearse and Connolly
He'd gone to great expense
Keeping all the Kerry men
Out of that crazy fight;
That he might be there himself
Had travelled half the night.
                    How goes the weather?

'Am I such a craven that
I should not get the word
But for what some travelling man
Had heard I had not heard?'
Then on Pearse and Connolly
He fixed a bitter look:
'Because I helped to wind the clock
I come to hear it strike.'
                    How goes the weather?

What remains to sing about
But of the death he met
Stretched under a doorway
Somewhere off Henry Street;
They that found him found upon
The door above his head
'Here died the O'Rahilly.
R.I.P.' writ in blood.
                    How goes the weather?

Come gather round me, Parnellites,
And praise our chosen man;
Stand upright on your legs awhile,
Stand upright while you can,
For soon we lie where he is laid,
And he is underground;
Come fill up all those glasses
And pass the bottle round.

And here's a cogent reason,
And I have many more,
He fought the might of England
And saved the Irish poor,
Whatever good a farmer's got
He brought it all to pass;
And here's another reason,
That Parnell loved a lass.

And here's a final reason,
He was of such a kind
Every man that sings a song
Keeps Parnell in his mind.
For Parnell was a proud man,
No prouder trod the ground,
And a proud man's a lovely man,
So pass the bottle round.

The Bishops and the Party
That tragic story made,
A husband that had sold his wife
And after that betrayed;
But stories that live longest
Are sung above the glass,
And Parnell loved his country,
And Parnell loved his lass.

I fasted for some forty days on bread and buttermilk,
For passing round the bottle with girls in rags or silk,
In country shawl or Paris cloak, had put my wits astray,
And what's the good of women, for all that they can say
Is fol de rol de rolly O.

Round Lough Derg's holy island I went upon the stones,
I prayed at all the Stations upon my marrow-bones,
And there I found an old man, and though I prayed all day
And that old man beside me, nothing would he say
But fol de rol de rolly O.

All know that all the dead in the world about that place are stuck,
And that should mother seek her son she'd have but little luck
Because the fires of Purgatory have ate their shapes away;
I swear to God I questioned them, and all they had to say
Was fol de rol de rolly O.

A great black ragged bird appeared when I was in the boat;
Some twenty feet from tip to tip had it stretched rightly out,
With flopping and with flapping it made a great display,
But I never stopped to question, what could the boatman say
But fol de rol de rolly O.

Now I am in the public-house and lean upon the wall,
So come in rags or come in silk, in cloak or country shawl,
And come with learned lovers or with what men you may,
For I can put the whole lot down, and all I have to say
Is fol de rol de rolly O.

*Lough Derg pilgrims on the mainland,
with the holy island in the background.*

I

Around me the images of thirty years:
An ambush; pilgrims at the water-side;
Casement upon trial, half hidden by the bars,
Guarded; Griffith staring in hysterical pride;
Kevin O'Higgins' countenance that wears
A gentle questioning look that cannot hide
A soul incapable of remorse or rest;
A revolutionary soldier kneeling to be blessed;

II

An Abbot or Archbishop with an upraised hand
Blessing the Tricolour. 'This is not,' I say,
'The dead Ireland of my youth, but an Ireland
The poets have imagined, terrible and gay.'
Before a woman's portrait suddenly I stand,
Beautiful and gentle in her Venetian way.
I met her all but fifty years ago
For twenty minutes in some studio.

III

Heart-smitten with emotion I sink down,
My heart recovering with covered eyes;
Wherever I had looked I had looked upon
My permanent or impermanent images:
Augusta Gregory's son; her sister's son,
Hugh Lane, 'onlie begetter' of all these;
Hazel Lavery living and dying, that tale
As though some ballad-singer had sung it all;

IV

Mancini's portrait of Augusta Gregory,
'Greatest since Rembrandt,' according to John Synge;
A great ebullient portrait certainly;
But where is the brush that could show anything
Of all that pride and that humility?
And I am in despair that time may bring
Approved patterns of women or of men
But not that selfsame excellence again.

V

My mediaeval knees lack health until they bend,
But in that woman, in that household where
Honour had lived so long, all lacking found.
Childless I thought, 'My children may find here
Deep-rooted things,' but never foresaw its end,
And now that end has come I have not wept;
No fox can foul the lair the badger swept —

VI

(An image out of Spenser and the common tongue).
John Synge, I and Augusta Gregory, thought
All that we did, all that we said or sang
Must come from contact with the soil, from that
Contact everything Antaeus-like grew strong.
We three alone in modern times had brought
Everything down to that sole test again,
Dream of the noble and the beggar-man.

VII

And here's John Synge himself, that rooted man,
'Forgetting human words,' a grave deep face.
You that would judge me, do not judge alone
This book or that, come to this hallowed place
Where my friends' portraits hang and look thereon;
Ireland's history in their lineaments trace;
Think where man's glory most begins and ends,
And say my glory was I had such friends.

'A revolutionary soldier kneeling to be blessed.'
THE BLESSING OF THE COLOURS
by Sir John Lavery.

A bloody and a sudden end,
    Gunshot or a noose,
For Death who takes what man would keep,
    Leaves what man would lose.
He might have had my sister,
    My cousins by the score,
But nothing satisfied the fool
    But my dear Mary Moore,
None other knows what pleasures man
    At table or in bed.
What shall I do for pretty girls
    Now my old bawd is dead?

Though stiff to strike a bargain,
    Like an old Jew man,
Her bargain struck we laughed and talked
    And emptied many a can;
And O! but she had stories,
    Though not for the priest's ear,
To keep the soul of man alive,
    Banish age and care,
And being old she put a skin
    On everything she said.
What shall I do for pretty girls
    Now my old bawd is dead?

The priests have got a book that says
    But for Adam's sin
Eden's Garden would be there
    And I there within.
No expectation fails there,
    No pleasing habit ends,
No man grows old, no girl grows cold,
    But friends walk by friends.
Who quarrels over halfpennies
    That plucks the trees for bread?
What shall I do for pretty girls
    Now my old bawd is dead?

Why should not old men be mad?
Some have known a likely lad
That had a sound fly-fisher's wrist
Turn to a drunken journalist;
A girl that knew all Dante once
Live to bear children to a dunce;
A Helen of social welfare dream,
Climb on a wagonette to scream.
Some think it a matter of course that chance
Should starve good men and bad advance,
That if their neighbours figured plain,
As though upon a lighted screen,
No single story would they find
Of an unbroken happy mind,
A finish worthy of the start.
Young men know nothing of this sort,
Observant old men know it well;
And when they know what old books tell,
And that no better can be had,
Know why an old man should be mad.

Jack B. Yeats drew his memory of the raving old
man who made a pulpit out of a rusty boiler on
Sligo Quay.

ON THE BOILER

By

W. B. YEATS

THE CUALA PRESS · DUBLIN

PRICE: THREE SHILLINGS AND SIXPENCE

CRAZY JANE ON THE MOUNTAIN

I am tired of cursing the Bishop,
(Said Crazy Jane)
Nine books or nine hats
Would not make him a man.
I have found something worse
To meditate on.
A King had some beautiful cousins,
But where are they gone?
Battered to death in a cellar,
And he stuck to his throne.
Last night I lay on the mountain,
(Said Crazy Jane)
There is a two-horsed carriage
That on two wheels ran
Great-bladdered Emer sat,
Her violent man
Cuchulain sat at her side;
Thereupon,
Propped upon my two knees,
I kissed a stone;
I lay stretched out in the dirt
And I cried tears down.

THE STATESMAN'S HOLIDAY

I lived among great houses,
Riches drove out rank,
Base drove out the better blood,
And mind and body shrank.
No Oscar ruled the table,
But I'd a troop of friends
That knowing better talk had gone
Talked of odds and ends.
Some knew what ailed the world
But never said a thing,
So I have picked a better trade
And night and morning sing:
Tall dames go walking in grass-green Avalon.

Am I a great Lord Chancellor
That slept upon the Sack?
Commanding officer that tore
The khaki from his back?
Or am I de Valéra,
Or the King of Greece,
Or the man that made the motors?
Ach, call me what you please!
Here's a Montenegrin lute,
And its old sole string
Makes me sweet music
And I delight to sing:
Tall dames go walking in grass-green Avalon.

With boys and girls about him,
With any sort of clothes,
With a hat out of fashion,
With old patched shoes,
With a ragged bandit cloak,
With an eye like a hawk,
With a stiff straight back,
With a strutting turkey walk,
With a bag full of pennies,
With a monkey on a chain,
With a great cock's feather,
With an old foul tune.
Tall dames go walking in grass-green Avalon.

I

I sought a theme and sought for it in vain,
I sought it daily for six weeks or so.
Maybe at last, being but a broken man,
I must be satisfied with my heart, although
Winter and summer till old age began
My circus animals were all on show,
Those stilted boys, that burnished chariot,
Lion and woman and the Lord knows what.

II

What can I but enumerate old themes?
First that sea-rider Oisin led by the nose
Through three enchanted islands, allegorical dreams,
Vain gaiety, vain battle, vain repose,
Themes of the embittered heart, or so it seems,
That might adorn old songs or courtly shows;
But what cared I that set him on to ride,
I, starved for the bosom of his faery bride?

And then a counter-truth filled out its play,
The Countess Cathleen was the name I gave it;
She, pity-crazed, had given her soul away,
But masterful Heaven had intervened to save it.
I thought my dear must her own soul destroy,
So did fanaticism and hate enslave it,
And this brought forth a dream and soon enough
This dream itself had all my thought and love.

And when the Fool and Blind Man stole the bread
Cuchulain fought the ungovernable sea;
Heart-mysteries there, and yet when all is said
It was the dream itself enchanted me:
Character isolated by a deed
To engross the present and dominate memory.
Players and painted stage took all my love,
And not those things that they were emblems of.

III

Those masterful images because complete
Grew in pure mind, but out of what began?
A mound of refuse or the sweepings of a street,
Old kettles, old bottles, and a broken can,
Old iron, old bones, old rags, that raving slut
Who keeps the till. Now that my ladder's gone,
I must lie down where all the ladders start,
In the foul rag-and-bone shop of the heart.

Charles Ricketts designed the costumes for the
Fool and Blindman in the dream and heart-mysteries
that enchanted the poet in the play On Baile's
Strand *(1915)*, his central contribution to the
Cuchulain saga.

I

Swear by what the sages spoke
Round the Mareotic Lake
That the Witch of Atlas knew,
Spoke and set the cocks a-crow.

Swear by those horsemen, by those women
Complexion and form prove superhuman,
That pale, long-visaged company
That air in immortality
Completeness of their passions won;
Now they ride the wintry dawn
Where Ben Bulben sets the scene.

Here's the gist of what they mean.

II

Many times man lives and dies
Between his two eternities,
That of race and that of soul,
And ancient Ireland knew it all.
Whether man die in his bed
Or the rifle knocks him dead,
A brief parting from those dear
Is the worst man has to fear.
Though grave-diggers' toil is long,
Sharp their spades, their muscles strong,
They but thrust their buried men
Back in the human mind again.

III

You that Mitchel's prayer have heard,
'Send war in our time, O Lord!'
Know that when all words are said
And a man is fighting mad,
Something drops from eyes long blind,
He completes his partial mind,
For an instant stands at ease,
Laughs aloud, his heart at peace.
Even the wisest man grows tense
With some sort of violence
Before he can accomplish fate,
Know his work or choose his mate.

IV

Poet and sculptor, do the work,
Nor let the modish painter shirk
What his great forefathers did,
Bring the soul of man to God,
Make him fill the cradles right.

Measurement began our might:
Forms a stark Egyptian thought,
Forms that gentler Phidias wrought.
Michael Angelo left a proof
On the Sistine Chapel roof,
Where but half-awakened Adam
Can disturb globe-trotting Madam
Till her bowels are in heat,
Proof that there's a purpose set
Before the secret working mind:
Profane perfection of mankind.

Quattrocento put in paint
On backgrounds for a God or Saint
Gardens where a soul's at ease;
Where everything that meets the eye,
Flowers and grass and cloudless sky,
Resemble forms that are or seem
When sleepers wake and yet still dream,
And when it's vanished still declare,
With only bed and bedstead there,
That heavens had opened.

                              Gyres run on;
When that greater dream had gone
Calvert and Wilson, Blake and Claude,
Prepared a rest for the people of God,
Palmer's phrase, but after that
Confusion fell upon our thought.

V

Irish poets, learn your trade,
Sing whatever is well made,
Scorn the sort now growing up
All out of shape from toe to top,
Their unremembering hearts and heads
Base-born products of base beds.
Sing the peasantry, and then
Hard-riding country gentlemen,
The holiness of monks, and after
Porter-drinkers' randy laughter;
Sing the lords and ladies gay
That were beaten into the clay
Through seven heroic centuries;
Cast your mind on other days
That we in coming days may be
Still the indomitable Irishry.

VI

Under bare Ben Bulben's head
In Drumcliff churchyard Yeats is laid.
An ancestor was rector there
Long years ago, a church stands near,
By the road an ancient cross.
No marble, no conventional phrase;
On limestone quarried near the spot
By his command these words are cut:

> *Cast a cold eye*
> *On life, on death.*
> *Horseman, pass by!*

September 4, 1938

*The ballad seller, an illustration by Jack B. Yeats
printed by The Cuala Press.*

MYTHOLOGIES

The great central edifice of the poet's prose stands on five pillars, or the works collected into *Autobiographies, Essays and Introductions, Mythologies, Explorations* and the volume of *Memoirs* edited by Denis Donoghue. They cover, as far as we may guess, almost every aspect of Yeats' life and thought, from his early interest in ancient lore and beliefs, through his life in London in the artistic world to which his father had introduced him, his tumultuous Dublin years in the creation of a national theatre and literary consciousness, and the politics of national resurgence, inextricably entangled with that 'barren passion' for a beautiful and fanatical woman.

There was, also, his consideration of other writers and artists, present and past, and of distinguished friends and public figures, of all living people and of life and the meaning thereof insofar as he, or anybody else, might guess at it.

Mythologies gathers together *The Celtic Twilight* (1893), *The Secret Rose* (1897) and *Stories of Red Hanrahan* (1897). Then into the mystical and occultist world, if world is the right word, in *Rosa Alchemica, The Tables of the Law,* and *The Adoration of the Magi* (1897) and *Per Amica Silentia Lunae* (1917).

In this way Yeats begins the collection *The Celtic Twilight*:

Many of the tales in this book were told me by one Paddy Flynn, a little, bright-eyed, old man, who lived in a leaky and one-roomed cabin in the village of Ballisodare, which is, he was wont to say, 'the most gentle' – whereby he meant, faery – 'place in the whole of County Sligo.' Others hold it, however, but second to Drumcliff and Dromahair. The first time I saw him he was bent above the fire with a can of mushrooms at his side; the next time he was asleep under a hedge, smiling in his sleep. He was indeed always cheerful, though I thought I could see in his eyes (swift as the eyes of a rabbit, when they peered out of their wrinkled holes) a melancholy which was well-nigh a portion of their joy: the visionary melancholy of purely instinctive natures and of all animals.

Then there follow many tales, and accounts of customs and beliefs with which anyone reared within hearing distance of rural Ireland, say, fifty or sixty years ago, or in some districts less time ago, should be readily familiar. All this may have, at some times and in some places, earned a dubious reputation for the Celtic twilight as the mist that does be on the bog.

But for me, two tales stand up as hard as rock and bright as celestial vision: one, 'Dust Hath Closed Helen's Eye' (p. 143) from the byroads of the counties of Galway and Clare or, to be exact, from the much-mentioned Ballylee of beauty and the blind poet; the other, The Last Gleeman (p. 148) from the shadowy streets of Old Dublin.

The trout spoke to the Munster poet, Aogán Ó Rathaille (c. 1675–1729), when he was crossing a stream, and told the poet not to tread on the trout: who was, I suspect, not pleading for pity but warning the poet to keep to his own territory.

Similarly the bush spoke to Blind Raftery to remind him that the bush was an old person and a long time in that place: one small but sharp point in a lengthy poem.

The image was to stay with Yeats and to illumine the wonderful 'Lamentation of the Old Pensioner' spitting into the face of transfiguring Time.

The verses which the young Yeats resurrects from the streets of Old Dublin are also blind and as crabbed as any thornbush twisting out of a drystone wall in faraway Connacht.

In an alternative ending to The Last Gleeman, Yeats saw Moran in some Middle Kingdom gathering around him a group of dishevelled angels. That was the first version of the essay I read, in 1934, and I have a fondness for it. But the poet may have dropped that ending out of a tenderness for some Irish writers either from his own present or from the past. Here we may, in all humility, restore it:

Moran must have felt strange and out of place in that other Kingdom he was entering, perhaps while his friends were drinking in his honour. Let us hope that some kindly middle region was found for him, where he can call dishevelled angels about him with some new and more rhythmical form of his old . . .

Gather round me, boys, will yez
  Gather round me?
And hear what I have to say
  Before ould Salley brings me
Me bread and jug of tay.

. . . and fling outrageous quips and cranks at cherubim and seraphim. Perhaps he may have found and gathered, ragamuffin though he be, the Lily of High Truth, the Rose of Far-sight Beauty, for whose lack so many of the writers of Ireland, whether famous or forgotten, have been futile as the blown froth upon the shore.

Red Hanrahan, the enchanted poet, Yeats considered he had himself created, and that he drove him 'drunk or sober through the dawn'. Hanrahan is a gigantic figure and almost certainly had a prototype in a Gaelic poet of the eighteenth century.

The stories about Hanrahan were written in 1897 and rewritten in 1907 'with Lady Gregory's help'. They range from his first crazy enchantment and through all his wanderings to the moment of his death.

Here we give only the first story, Red Hanrahan (p. 152), but there is enough magic in it to draw any reader 'caught by an old man's juggleries' to follow on to the final moment:

When the sun rose on the morning of the morrow, Winny of the Cross-Roads rose up from where she was sitting beside the body, and began her begging from townland to townland, singing the same song as she walked: 'I am beautiful, I am beautiful. The birds in the air, the moths under the leaves, the flies over the water look at me. I am young: look upon me, mountains; look upon me, perishing woods, for my body will be shining like the white waters when you have been hurried away. You and the whole race of men, and the race of the beasts, and the race of the fish, and the winged race, are dropping like a candle that is nearly burned out. But I laugh aloud because I am in my youth.'

She did not come back that night or any night to the cabin, and it was not till the end of two days that the turf-cutters going to the bog found the body of Red Owen Hanrahan, and gathered men to wake him and women to keen him, and gave him a burying worthy of so great a poet.

'DUST HATH CLOSED HELEN'S EYE'

I

I HAVE been lately to a little group of houses, not many enough to be called a village, in the barony of Kiltartan in County Galway, whose name, Ballylee, is known through all the west of Ireland. There is the old square castle,[*] Ballylee, inhabited by a farmer and his wife, and a cottage where their daughter and their son-in-law live, and a little mill with an old miller, and old ash-trees throwing green shadows upon a little river and great stepping-stones. I went there two or three times last year to talk to the miller about Biddy Early, a wise woman that lived in Clare some years ago, and about her saying, 'There is a cure for all evil between the two mill-wheels of Ballylee,' and to find out from him or another whether she meant the moss between the running waters or some other herb. I have been there this summer, and I shall be there again before it is autumn, because Mary Hynes, a beautiful woman whose name is still a wonder by turf fires, died there sixty years ago; for our feet would linger where beauty has lived its life of sorrow to make us understand that it is not of the world. An old man brought me a little way from the mill and the castle, and down a long, narrow boreen that was nearly lost in brambles and sloe-bushes, and he said, 'That is the little old foundation of the house, but the most of it is taken for building walls, and the goats have ate those bushes that are growing over it till they've got cranky, and they won't grow any more. They say she was the handsomest girl in Ireland, her skin was like dribbled snow'—he meant driven snow, perhaps—'and she had blushes in her cheeks. She had five handsome brothers, but all are gone now!' I talked to him about a poem in Irish, Raftery, a famous poet, made about her, and how it said, 'There is a strong cellar in Ballylee.' He said the strong cellar was the great hole where the river sank underground, and he brought me to a deep pool, where an otter hurried away under a grey boulder, and told me that many fish came up out of the dark water at early morning 'to taste the fresh water coming down from the hills'.

I first heard of the poem from an old woman who lives about two miles farther up the river, and who remembers Raftery and Mary Hynes. She says, 'I never saw anybody so handsome as she was, and I never will till I die,' and that he was nearly blind, and had 'no way of living but to go round and to mark some house to go to, and then all the neighbours would gather to hear. If you treated him well he'd praise you, but if you did not, he'd fault you in Irish. He was the greatest poet in Ireland, and he'd make a song about that bush if he chanced to stand under it. There was a bush he stood under

---

[*] Ballylee Castle, or Thoor Ballylee, as I have named it to escape from the too magnificent word 'castle,' is now my property, and I spend my summers or some part of them there. (1924.)

from the rain, and he made verses praising it, and then when the water came through he made verses dispraising it.' She sang the poem to a friend and to myself in Irish, and every word was audible and expressive, as the words in a song were always, as I think, before music grew too proud to be the garment of words, flowing and changing with the flowing and changing of their energies. The poem is not as natural as the best Irish poetry of the last century, for the thoughts are arranged in a too obviously traditional form, so the old poor half-blind man who made it has to speak as if he were a rich farmer offering the best of everything to the woman he loves, but it has naïve and tender phrases. The friend that was with me has made some of the translation, but some of it has been made by the country people themselves. I think it has more of the simplicity of the Irish verses than one finds in most translations.

Going to Mass by the will of God,
The day came wet and the wind rose;
I met Mary Hynes at the cross of Kiltartan,
And I fell in love with her then and there.

I spoke to her kind and mannerly,
As by report was her own way;
And she said, 'Raftery, my mind is easy,
You may come to-day to Ballylee.'

When I heard her offer I did not linger,
When her talk went to my heart my heart rose.
We had only to go across the three fields,
We had daylight with us to Ballylee.

The table was laid with glasses and a quart measure,
She had fair hair, and she sitting beside me;
And she said, 'Drink, Raftery, and a hundred welcomes,
There is a strong cellar in Ballylee.'

O star of light and O sun in harvest,
O amber hair, O my share of the world,
Will you come with me upon Sunday
Till we agree together before all the people?

I would not grudge you a song every Sunday evening,
Punch on the table, or wine if you would drink it,
But, O King of Glory, dry the roads before me
Till I find the way to Ballylee.

There is sweet air on the side of the hill
When you are looking down upon Ballylee;
When you are walking in the valley picking nuts and blackberries,
There is music of the birds in it and music of the Sidhe.

What is the worth of greatness till you have the light
Of the flower of the branch that is by your side?
There is no god to deny it or to try and hide it,
She is the sun in the heavens who wounded my heart.

There was no part of Ireland I did not travel,
From the rivers to the tops of the mountains,
To the edge of Lough Greine whose mouth is hidden,
And I saw no beauty but was behind hers.

Her hair was shining, and her brows were shining too;
Her face was like herself, her mouth pleasant and sweet.
She is the pride, and I give her the branch,
She is the shining flower of Ballylee.

It is Mary Hynes, the calm and easy woman,
Has beauty in her mind and in her face.
If a hundred clerks were gathered together,
They could not write down a half of her ways.

An old weaver, whose son is supposed to go away among the Sidhe (the faeries) at night, says, 'Mary Hynes was the most beautiful thing ever made. My mother used to tell me about her, for she'd be at every hurling, and wherever she was she dressed in white. As many as eleven men asked her in marriage in one day, but she wouldn't have any of them. There was a lot of men up beyond Kilbecanty one night sitting together drinking, and talking of her, and one of them got up and set out to go to Ballylee and see her; but Cloone Bog was open then, and when he came to it he fell into the water, and they found him dead there in the morning. She died of the fever that was before the famine.' Another old man says he was only a child when he saw her, but he remembered that 'the strongest man that was among us, one John Madden, got his death of the head of her, cold he got crossing rivers in the night-time to get to Ballylee.' This is perhaps the man the other remembered, for tradition gives the one thing many shapes. There is an old woman who remembers her, at Derrybrien among the Echtge hills, a vast desolate place, which has changed little since the old poem said, 'the stag upon the cold summit of Echtge hears the cry of the wolves,' but still mindful of many poems and of the dignity of ancient speech. She says, 'The sun and the moon never shone on anybody so handsome, and her skin was so white that it looked blue, and she had two little blushes on her cheeks.' And an old wrinkled woman who lives close by Ballylee, and has told me many tales of the Sidhe, says, 'I often saw Mary Hynes, she was handsome indeed. She had two bunches of curls beside her cheeks, and they were the colour of silver. I saw Mary Molloy that was drowned in the river beyond, and Mary Guthrie that was in Ardrahan, but she took the sway of them both, a very comely creature. I was at her wake too – she had seen too much of the world. She was a kind creature. One day I was coming home through that field beyond, and I was tired, and who should come out but the Poisin Glegeal (the shining flower), and she gave me a glass of new milk.' This old woman meant no more than some beautiful bright colour by the colour of silver, for though I knew an old man – he is dead now – who thought she might know 'the cure for all the evils in the world,' that the Sidhe knew, she has seen too little gold to know its colour. But a man by the shore at Kinvara, who is too young to remember Mary Hynes, says, 'Everybody says there is no one at all to be seen now so handsome; it is said she had beautiful hair, the colour of gold. She was poor, but her clothes every day were the same as Sunday, she had such neatness. And if she went to any kind of a meeting, they would all be killing one another for a sight of her, and there was a great many in love with her, but she died young. It is said that no one that has a song made about them will ever live long.'

Those who are much admired are, it is held, taken by the Sidhe, who can use ungoverned feeling for their own ends, so that a father, as an old herb-doctor told me once, may give his child into their hands, or a husband his wife. The admired and desired are only safe if one says 'God bless them' when one's eyes are upon them. The old woman that sang the song thinks, too, that Mary Hynes was 'taken,' as the phrase is, 'for they have taken many that are not handsome, and why would they not take her? And people came from all parts to look at her, and maybe there were some that did not say "God bless her."' An old man who lives by the sea at Duras has as little doubt that she was taken, 'for there are some living yet can remember her coming to the pattern* there beyond, and she was said to be the handsomest girl in Ireland.' She died young because the gods loved her, for the Sidhe are the gods, and it may be that the old saying, which we forget to understand literally, meant her manner of death in old times. These poor countrymen and countrywomen in their beliefs, and in their emotions, are many years nearer to that old Greek world, that set beauty beside the fountain of things, than are our men of learning. She 'had seen too much of the world'; but

* A 'pattern', or 'patron', is a festival in honour of a saint.

146

these old men and women, when they tell of her, blame another and not her, and though they can be hard, they grow gentle as the old men of Troy grew gentle when Helen passed by on the walls.

The poet who helped her to so much fame has himself a great fame throughout the west of Ireland. Some think that Raftery was half blind, and say, 'I saw Raftery, a dark man, but he had sight enough to see her,' or the like, but some think he was wholly blind, as he may have been at the end of his life. Fable makes all things perfect in their kind, and her blind people must never look on the world and the sun. I asked a man I met one day, when I was looking for a pool *na mna Sidhe* where women of Faery have been seen, how Raftery could have admired Mary Hynes so much if he had been altogether blind. He said, 'I think Raftery was altogether blind, but those that are blind have a way of seeing things, and have the power to know more, and to feel more, and to do more, and to guess more than those that have their sight, and a certain wit and a certain wisdom is given to them.' Everybody, indeed, will tell you that he was very wise, for was he not not only blind but a poet? The weaver, whose words about Mary Hynes I have already given, says, 'His poetry was the gift of the Almighty, for there are three things that are the gift of the Almighty — poetry and dancing and principles. That is why in the old times an ignorant man coming down from the hillside would be better behaved and have better learning than a man with education you'd meet now, for they got it from God'; and a man at Coole says, 'When he put his finger to one part of his head, everything would come to him as if it was written in a book'; and an old pensioner at Kiltartan says, 'He was standing under a bush one time, and he talked to it, and it answered him back in Irish. Some say it was the bush that spoke, but it must have been an enchanted voice in it, and it gave him the knowledge of all the things of the world. The bush withered up afterwards, and it is to be seen on the roadside now between this and Rahasine.' There is a poem of his about a bush, which I have never seen, and it may have come out of the cauldron of Fable in this shape.

A friend of mine met a man once who had been with him when he died, but the people say that he died alone, and one Maurteen Gillane told Dr Hyde that all night long a light was seen streaming up to heaven from the roof of the house where he lay, and 'that was the angels who were with him'; and all night long there was a great light in the hovel, 'and that was the angels who were waking him. They gave that honour to him because he was so good a poet, and sang such religious songs.' It may be that in a few years Fable, who changes mortalities to immortalities in her cauldron, will have changed Mary Hynes and Raftery to perfect symbols of the sorrow of beauty and of the magnificence and penury of dreams.

1900

When I was in a northern town a while ago I had a long talk with a man who had lived in a neighbouring country district when he was a boy. He told me that when a very beautiful girl was born in a family that had not been noted for good looks, her beauty was thought to have come from the Sidhe, and to bring misfortune with it. He went over the names of several beautiful girls that he had known, and said that beauty had never brought happiness to anybody. It was a thing, he said, to be proud of and afraid of. I wish I had written out his words at the time, for they were more picturesque than my memory of them.

1902

THE LAST GLEEMAN

MICHAEL MORAN was born about 1794 off Black Pitts, in the Liberties of Dublin, in Faddle Alley. A fortnight after birth he went stone blind from illness, and became thereby a blessing to his parents, who were soon able to send him to rhyme and beg at street corners and at the bridges over the Liffey. They may well have wished that their quiver were full of such as he, for, free from the interruption of sight, his mind turned every movement of the day and every change of public passion into rhyme or quaint saying. By the time he had grown to manhood he was the admitted rector of all the ballad-mongers of the Liberties, of Madden, the weaver, Kearney, the blind fiddler from Wicklow, Martin from Meath, M'Bride from Heaven knows where, and that M'Grane, who in after days, when the true Moran was no more, strutted in borrowed plumes, or rather in borrowed rags, and gave out that there had never been any Moran but himself, and many another. Nor despite his blindness did he find any difficulty in getting a wife, but rather was able to pick and choose, for he was just that mixture of ragamuffin and of genius which is dear to the heart of woman, who, however conventional in herself, loves the unexpected, the crooked, the bewildering. Nor did he lack, despite his rags, many excellent things, for it is remembered that he ever loved caper sauce, and upon one occasion when his wife had forgotten it, he flung a leg of mutton at her head. He was not, certainly, much to look at, with his coarse frieze coat with its cape and scalloped edge, his old corduroy trousers and great brogues, and his stout stick made fast to his wrist by a thong of leather: and he would have been a woeful shock to the gleeman MacCoinglinne, could that friend of kings have beheld him in prophetic vision from the pillar stone at

Cork. And yet though the short cloak and the leather wallet were no more, he was a true gleeman, being alike poet, jester, and newsman of the people. In the morning when he had finished his breakfast, his wife or some neighbour would read the newspaper to him, and read on and on until he interrupted with, 'That'll do – I have me meditations'; and from these meditations would come the day's store of jest and rhyme. He had the whole Middle Ages under his frieze coat.

He had not, however, MacCoinglinne's hatred of the Church and clergy, for when the fruit of his meditations did not ripen well, or when the crowd called for something more solid, he would recite or sing a metrical tale or ballad of saint or martyr or some Biblical adventure. He would stand at a street corner, and when a crowd had gathered would begin in some such fashion as follows (I copy the record of one who knew him): – 'Gather round me, boys, gather round me. Boys, am I standin' in puddle? am I standin' in wet?' Thereon several boys would cry, 'Ah, no! yez not! yer in a nice dry place. Go on with *Saint Mary*; go on with *Moses*' – each calling for his favourite tale. Then Moran, with a wriggle of his body and a clutch at his rags, would burst out with, 'All me buzzim friends are turned backbiters'; and after a final warning to the boys, 'If yez don't drop your coddin' and diversion I'll lave some of yez a case,' begin his recitation, or perhaps still delay, to ask, 'Is there a crowd round me now? Any blaguard heretic around me?' Or he would, it may be, start by singing: –

Gather round me, boys, will yez
  Gather round me?
And hear what I have to say
  Before ould Sally brings me
My bread and jug of tay.

The best-known of his religious tales was *Saint Mary of Egypt*, a long poem of exceeding solemnity, condensed from the much longer work of a certain Bishop Coyle. It told how an Egyptian harlot, Mary by name, followed pilgrims to Jerusalem in pursuit of her trade, and then, on finding herself withheld from entering the Temple by supernatural interference, turned penitent, fled to the desert and spent the remainder of her life in solitary penance. When at last she was at the point of death, God sent Bishop Zosimus to hear her confession, give her the last sacrament, and with the help of a lion, whom He sent also, dig her grave. The poem has the intolerable cadence of the eighteenth century at its worst, but was so popular and so often called for that Moran was nicknamed Zosimus, and by that name is he remembered. He had also a poem of his own called *Moses*, which went a little nearer poetry without going very near. But he could ill brook solemnity, and before long parodied his own verses in the following ragamuffin fashion: –

In Egypt's land, contagious to the Nile,
King Pharaoh's daughter went to bathe in style.
She tuk her dip, then walked unto the land,
To dry her royal pelt she ran along the strand.
A bulrush tripped her, whereupon she saw
A smiling babby in a wad o' straw.
She tuk it up, and said with accents mild,
"Tare-and-agers, girls, which av yez owns the child?'

His humorous rhymes were, however, more often quips and cranks at the expense of his contemporaries. It was his delight, for instance, to remind a shoemaker, noted alike for display of wealth and for personal uncleanness, of his inconsiderable origin in a song of which but the first stanza has come down to us: —

At the dirty end of Dirty Lane,
Liv'd a dirty cobbler, Dick Maclane;
His wife was in the old King's reign
    A stout brave orange-woman.
On Essex Bridge she strained her throat,
And six-a-penny was her note.
But Dickey wore a bran-new coat
    He got among the yeomen.
He was a bigot, like his clan,
And in the streets he wildly sang,
O Roly, toly, toly raid, with his old jade.

He had troubles of divers kinds, and numerous interlopers to face and put down. Once an officious peeler arrested him as a vagabond, but was triumphantly routed amid the laughter of the court, when Moran reminded his worship of the precedent set by Homer, who was also, he declared, a poet, and a blind man, and a beggar-man. He had to face a more serious difficulty as his fame grew. Various imitators started up upon all sides. A certain actor, for instance, made as many guineas as Moran did shillings by mimicking his sayings and his songs and his get-up upon the stage. One night this actor was at supper with some friends, when dispute arose as to whether his mimicry was overdone or not. It was agreed to settle it by an appeal to the mob. A forty-shilling supper at a famous coffee-house was to be the wager. The actor took up his station at Essex Bridge, a great haunt of Moran's, and soon gathered a small crowd. He had scarce got through 'In Egypt's land, contagious to the Nile', when Moran himself came up, followed by another crowd. The crowds met in great excitement and laughter.

'Good Christians,' cried the pretender, 'is it possible that any man would mock the poor dark man like that?'

'Who's that? It's some imposhterer,' replied Moran.

'Begone, you wretch! it's you'se the imposhterer. Don't you fear the light of heaven being struck from your eyes for mocking the poor dark man?'

'Saints and angels, is there no protection against this? You're a most inhuman blaguard to try to deprive me of my honest bread this way,' replied poor Moran.

'And you, you wretch, won't let me go on with the beautiful poem? Christian people, in your charity won't you beat this man away? he's taking advantage of my darkness.'

The pretender, seeing that he was having the best of it, thanked the people for their sympathy and protection, and went on with the poem, Moran listening for a time in bewildered silence. After a while Moran protested again with: —

'Is it possible that none of yez can know me? Don't yez see it's myself; and that's some one else?'

'Before I can proceed any further in this lovely story,' interrupted the pretender, 'I call on yez to contribute your charitable donations to help me to go on.'

'Have you no sowl to be saved, you mocker of Heaven?' cried Moran, put completely beside himself by this last injury. 'Would you rob the poor as well as desave the world? O, was ever such wickedness known?'

'I leave it to yourselves, my friends,' said the pretender, 'to give to the real dark man, that you all know so well, and save me from that schemer,' and with that he collected some pennies and halfpence. While he was doing so, Moran started his *Mary of Egypt*, but the indignant crowd seizing his stick were about to belabour him, when they fell back bewildered anew by his close resemblance to himself. The pretender now called to them to 'just give him a grip of that villain, and he'd soon let him know who the imposhterer was!' They led him over to Moran, but instead of closing with him he thrust a few shillings into his hand, and turning to the crowd explained to them he was indeed but an actor, and that he had just gained a wager, and so departed amid much enthusiasm, to eat the supper he had won.

In April 1846 word was sent to the priest that Michael Moran was dying. He found him at 15 (now 14½) Patrick Street, on a straw bed, in a room full of ragged ballad-singers come to cheer his last moments. After his death the ballad-singers, with many fiddles and the like, came again and gave him a fine wake, each adding to the merriment whatever he knew in the way of rann, tale, old saw, or quaint rhyme. He had had his day, had said his prayers and made his confession, and why should they not give him a hearty send-off? The funeral took place the next day. A good party of his admirers and friends got into the hearse with the coffin, for the day was wet and nasty. They had not gone far when one of them burst out with, 'It's cruel cowld, isn't it?' 'Garra',' replied another, 'we'll all be as stiff as the corpse when we get to the berrin'-ground.' 'Bad cess to him,' said a third; 'I wish he'd held out another month until the weather got dacent.' A man called Carroll thereupon produced a half-pint of whiskey, and they all drank to the soul of the departed. Unhappily, however, the hearse was overweighted, and they had not reached the cemetery before the spring broke, and the bottle with it.

RED HANRAHAN

HANRAHAN, THE HEDGE SCHOOLMASTER, a tall, strong, red-haired young man, came into the barn where some of the men of the village were sitting on Samhain Eve. It had been a dwelling-house, and when the man that owned it had built a better one, he had put the two rooms together, and kept it for a place to store one thing or another. There was a fire on the old hearth, and there were dip candles stuck in bottles, and there was a black quart bottle upon some boards that had been put across two barrels to make a table. Most of the men were sitting beside the fire, and one of them was singing a long wandering song, about a Munster man and a Connacht man that were quarrelling about their two provinces.

Hanrahan went to the man of the house and said, 'I got your message'; but when he had said that, he stopped, for an old mountainy man that had a shirt and trousers of unbleached flannel, and that was sitting by himself near the door, was looking at him, and moving an old pack of cards about in his hands and muttering. 'Don't mind him,' said the man of the house; 'he is only some stranger came in a while ago, and we bade him welcome, it being Samhain night, but I think he is not in his right wits. Listen to him now and you will hear what he is saying.'

They listened then, and they could hear the old man muttering to himself as he turned the cards, 'Spades and Diamonds, Courage and Power; Clubs and Hearts, Knowledge and Pleasure.'

'That is the kind of talk he has been going on with for the last hour,' said the man of the house, and Hanrahan turned his eyes from the old man as if he did not like to be looking at him.

'I got your message,' Hanrahan said then. '"He is in the barn with his three first cousins from Kilchriest," the messenger said, "and there are some neighbours with them."'

'It is my cousin over there is wanting to see you,' said the man of the house, and he called over a young frieze-coated man, who was listening to the song, and said, 'This is Red Hanrahan you have the message for.'

'It is a kind message, indeed,' said the young man, 'for it comes from your sweetheart, Mary Lavelle.'

'How would you get a message from her, and what do you know of her?'

'I don't know her, indeed, but I was in Loughrea yesterday, and a neighbour of hers that had some dealings with me was saying that she bade him send you word, if he met any one from this side in the market, that her mother has died from her, and if you have a mind yet to join with herself, she is willing to keep her word to you.'

'I will go to her indeed,' said Hanrahan.

'And she bade you make no delay, for if she has not a man in the house before the month is out, it is likely the little bit of land will be given to another.'

When Hanrahan heard that, he rose up from the bench he had sat down on. 'I will make no delay indeed,' he said; 'there is a full moon, and if I get as far as Kilchriest to-night, I will reach to her before the setting of the sun to-morrow.'

When the others heard that, they began to laugh at him for being in such haste to go to his sweetheart, and one asked him if he would leave his school in the old lime-kiln, where he was giving the children such good learning. But he said the children would be glad enough in the morning to find the place empty, and no one to keep them at their task; and as for his school he could set it up again in any place, having as he had his little inkpot hanging from his neck by a chain, and his big Virgil and his primer in the skirt of his coat.

Some of them asked him to drink a glass before he went, and a young man caught hold of his coat, and said he must not leave them without singing the song he had made in praise of Venus and of Mary Lavelle. He drank a glass of whiskey, but he said he would not stop but would set out on his journey.

'There's time enough, Red Hanrahan,' said the man of the house, 'It will be time enough for you to give up sport when you are after your marriage, and it might be a long time before we will see you again.'

'I will not stop,' said Hanrahan; 'my mind would be on the roads all the time, bringing me to the woman that sent for me, and she lonesome and watching till I come.'

Some of the others came about him, pressing him that had been such a pleasant comrade, so full of songs and every kind of trick and fun, not to leave them till the night would be over, but he refused them all, and shook them off, and went to the door. But as he put his foot over the threshold, the strange old man stood up and put his hand that was thin and withered like a bird's claw on Hanrahan's hand, and said: 'It is not Hanrahan, the learned man and the great songmaker, that should go out from a gathering like this, on a Samhain night. And stop here, now,' he said, 'and play a hand with me; and here is an old pack of cards has done its work many a night before this, and old as it is, there has been much of the riches of the world lost and won over it.'

One of the young men said, 'It isn't much of the riches of the world has stopped with yourself, old man,' and he looked at the old man's bare feet, and they all laughed. But Hanrahan did not laugh, but he sat down very quietly, without a word. Then one of them said, 'So you will stop with us after all, Hanrahan'; and the old man said, 'He will stop indeed, did you not hear me asking him?'

They all looked at the old man then as if wondering where he came from. 'It is far I am come,' he said; 'through France I have come, and through Spain, and by Lough Greine of the hidden mouth, and none has refused me anything.' And then he was silent and nobody liked to question him, and they began to play. There were six men at the boards playing, and the others were looking on behind. They played two or three games for nothing, and then the old man took a fourpenny bit, worn very thin and smooth, out from his pocket, and he called to the rest to put something on the game. Then they all put down something on the boards, and little as it was it looked much, from the way it was shoved from one to another, first one man winning it and then his neighbour. And sometimes the luck would go against a man and he would have nothing left, and then one or another would lend him something, and he would pay it again out of his winnings, for neither good nor bad luck stopped long with any one.

And once Hanrahan said as a man would say in a dream, 'It is time for me to be going the road'; but just then a good card came to him, and he played it out, and all the money began to come to him. And once he thought of Mary Lavelle, and he sighed; and that time his luck went from him, and he forgot her again.

But at last the luck went to the old man and it stayed with him, and all they had flowed into him, and he began to laugh little laughs to himself, and to sing over and over to himself, 'Spades and Diamonds, Courage and Power,' and so on, as if it was a verse of a song.

And after a while any one looking at the men, and seeing the way their bodies were rocking to and fro, and the way they kept their eyes on the old man's hands, would think they had drink taken, or that the whole store they had in the world was put on the cards; but that was not so, for the quart bottle had not been disturbed since the game began, and was nearly full yet, and all that was on the game was a few sixpenny bits and shillings, and maybe a handful of coppers.

'You are good men to win and good men to lose,' said the old man; 'you have play in your hearts.' He began then to shuffle the cards and to mix them, very quick and fast, till at last they could not see them to be cards at all, but you would think him to be making rings of fire in the air, as little lads would make them with whirling a lighted stick; and after that it seemed to them that all the room was dark, and they could see nothing but his hands and the cards.

And all in a minute a hare made a leap out from between his hands, and whether it was one of the cards that took that shape, or whether it was made out of nothing in the palms of his hands, nobody knew, but there it was running on the floor of the barn, as quick as any hare that ever lived.

Some looked at the hare, but more kept their eyes on the old man, and while they were looking at him a hound made a leap out between his hands, the same way as the hare did, and after that another hound and another, till there was a whole pack of them following the hare round and round the barn.

The players were all standing up now, with their backs to the boards, shrinking from the hounds, and nearly deafened with the noise of their yelping, but as quick as the hounds were they could not overtake the hare, but it went round, till at the last it seemed as if a blast of wind burst open the barn door, and the hare doubled and made a leap over the boards where the men had been playing, and went out of the door and away through the night, and the hounds over the boards and through the door after it.

Then the old man called out, 'Follow the hounds, follow the hounds, and it is a great hunt you will see to-night,' and he went out after them. But used as the men were to go hunting after hares, and ready as they were for any sport, they were in dread to go out into the night, and it was only Hanrahan that rose up and that said, 'I will follow, I will follow on.'

'You had best stop here, Hanrahan,' the young man that was nearest him said, 'for you might be going into some great danger.' But Hanrahan said, 'I will see fair play, I will see fair play,' and he went stumbling out of the door like a man in a dream, and the door shut after him as he went.

He thought he saw the old man in front of him, but it was only his own shadow that the full moon cast on the road before him, but he could hear the hounds crying after the hare over the wide green fields of Granagh, and he followed them very fast, for there was nothing to stop him; and after a while he came to smaller fields that had little walls of loose stones around them, and he threw the stones down as he crossed them, and did not wait to put them up again; and he passed by the place where the river goes underground at Ballylee, and he could hear the hounds going before him up towards the head of the river. Soon he found it harder to run, for it was uphill he was going, and clouds came over the moon, and it was hard for him to see his way, and once he left the path to take a short-cut, but his foot slipped into a bog-hole and he had to come back to it. And how long he was going he did not know, or what way he went, but at last he was up on the bare mountain, with nothing but the rough heather about him, and he could neither hear the hounds nor any other thing. But their cry began to come to him again, at first far off and then very near, and when it came quite close to him, it went up all of a sudden into the air, and there was the sound of hunting over his head; then it went away northward till he could hear nothing at all. 'That's not fair,' he said, 'that's not fair.' And he could walk no longer, but sat down on the heather where he was, in the heart of Slieve Echtge, for all the strength had gone from him, with the dint of the long journey he had made.

And after a while he took notice that there was a door close to him, and a light coming from it, and he wondered that being so close to him he had not seen it before. And he rose up, and tired as he was he went in at the door, and although it was night-time outside, it was daylight he found within. And presently he met with an old man that had been gathering summer thyme and yellow flag-flowers, and it seemed as if all the sweet smells of the summer were with them. And the old man said, 'It is a long time you have been coming to us, Hanrahan the learned man and the great songmaker.'

And with that he brought him into a very big shining house, and every grand thing Hanrahan had ever heard of, and every colour he had ever seen, was in it. There was a high place at the end of the house, and on it there was sitting in a high chair a woman, the most beautiful the world ever saw, having a long pale face and flowers about it, but she had the tired look of one that had been long waiting. And there were sitting on the step below her chair four grey old women, and the one of them was holding a great cauldron in her lap; and another a great stone on her knees, and heavy as it was it seemed light to her; and another of them had a very long spear that was made of pointed wood; and the last of them had a sword that was without a scabbard.

Hanrahan stood looking at them for a long time, but none of them spoke any word to him or looked at him at all. And he had it in his mind to ask who that woman in the chair was, that was like a queen, and what she was waiting for; but ready as he was with his tongue and afraid of no person, he was in dread now to speak to so beautiful a woman, and in so grand a place. And then he thought to ask what were the four things the four grey old women were holding like great treasures, but he could not think of the right words to bring out.

Then the first of the old women rose up, holding the cauldron between her two hands, and she said, 'Pleasure,' and Hanrahan said no word. Then the second old woman rose up with the stone in her hands, and she said, 'Power'; and the third old woman rose up with a spear in her hand, and she said, 'Courage'; and the last of the old women rose up having the sword in her hands, and she said, 'Knowledge.' And every one, after she had spoken, waited as if for Hanrahan to question her, but he said nothing at all. And then the four old women went out of the door, bringing their four treasures with them, and as they went out one of them said, 'He has no wish for us'; and another said, 'He is weak, he is weak'; and another said, 'He is afraid'; and the last said, 'His wits are gone from him.' And then they all said, 'Echtge, daughter of the Silver Hand, must stay in her sleep. It is a pity, it is a great pity.'

And then the woman that was like a queen gave a very sad sigh, and it seemed to Hanrahan as if the sigh had the sound in it of hidden streams; and if the place he was in had been ten times grander and more shining than it was, he could not have hindered sleep from coming on him; and he staggered like a drunken man and lay down there and then.

When Hanrahan awoke, the sun was shining on his face, but there was white frost on the grass around him, and there was ice on the edge of the stream he was lying by, and that goes running on through Doire-caol and Drim-na-rod. He knew by the shape of the hills and by the shining of Lough Greine in the distance that he was upon one of the hills of Slieve Echtge, but he was not sure how he came there; for all that had happened in the barn had gone from him, and all of his journey but the soreness of his feet and the stiffness in his bones.

It was a year after that, there were men of the village of Cappaghtagle sitting by the fire in a house on the roadside, and Red Hanrahan that was now very thin and worn, and his hair very long and wild, came to the half-door and asked leave to come in and rest himself; and they bid him welcome because it was Samhain night. He sat down with them, and they gave him a glass of whiskey out of a quart bottle; and they saw the little inkpot hanging about his neck, and knew he was a scholar, and asked for stories about the Greeks.

He took the Virgil out of the big pocket of his coat, but the cover was very black and swollen with the wet, and the page when he opened it was very yellow, but that was no great matter, for he looked at it like a man that had never learned to read. Some young man that was there began to laugh at him then, and to ask why did he carry so heavy a book with him when he was not able to read it.

It vexed Hanrahan to hear that, and he put the Virgil back in his pocket and asked if they had a pack of cards among them, for cards were better than books. When they brought out the cards he took them and began to shuffle them, and while he was shuffling them something seemed to come into his mind, and he put his hand to his face like one that is trying to remember, and he said, 'Was I ever here before, or where was I on a night like this?' and then of a sudden he stood up and let the cards fall to the floor, and he said, 'Who was it brought me a message from Mary Lavelle?'

'We never saw you before now, and we never heard of Mary Lavelle,' said the man of the house. 'And who is she,' he said, 'and what is it you are talking about?'

'It was this night a year ago, I was in a barn, and there were men playing cards, and there was money on the table, they were pushing it from one to another here and there — and I got a message, and I was going out of the door to look for my sweetheart that wanted me, Mary Lavelle.' And then Hanrahan called out very loud, 'Where have I been since then? Where was I for the whole year?'

'It is hard to say where you might have been in that time,' said the oldest of the men, 'or what part of the world you may have travelled; and it is like enough you have the dust of many roads on your feet; for there are many go wandering and forgetting like that,' he said, 'when once they have been given the touch.'

'That is true,' said another of the men. 'I knew a woman went wandering like that through the length of seven years; she came back after, and she told her friends she had often been glad enough to eat the food that was put in the pig's trough. And it is best for you to go to the priest now,' he said, 'and let him take off you whatever may have been put upon you.'

'It is to my sweetheart I will go, to Mary Lavelle,' said Hanrahan; 'it is too long I have delayed, how do I know what might have happened her in the length of a year?'

He was going out of the door then, but they all told him it was best for him to stop the night, and to get strength for the journey; and indeed he wanted that, for he was very weak, and when they gave him food he ate it like a man that had never seen food before, and one of them said, 'He is eating as if he had trodden on the hungry grass.' It was in the white light of the morning he set out, and the time seemed long to him till he could get to Mary Lavelle's house. But when he came to it, he found the door broken, and the thatch dropping from the roof, and no living person to be seen. And when he asked the neighbours what had happened her, all they could say was that she had been put out of the house, and had married some labouring man, and they had gone looking for work to London or Liverpool or some big place. And whether she found a worse place or a better he never knew, but anyway he never met with her or with news of her again.

AUTOBIOGRAPHIES

MO
NO
CE
RO
S
DE
AS
TR
I
S

THE CUALA PRESS
CHURCHTOWN
DUNDRUM
MCMXV

The *Autobiographies* begin, aptly enough, with the *Reveries Over Childhood and Youth*. Then follow the five books of *The Trembling of the Veil: Four Years: 1887–1891, Ireland After Parnell, Hodos Chameliontos, The Tragic Generation* and *The Stirring of the Bones*.

Then comes *Dramatis Personae*, covering the years 1896–1902 and the conflicts that went with, and the friendships that made possible – and, perhaps, the final triumph that came from the creating of – a national theatre.

Next follows *Estrangement: Extracts from a Diary Kept in 1909*. And then, most movingly, *The Death of Synge*, also extracts from that same diary. And finally *The Bounty of Sweden*, Yeats' account, among other things, of his journey to Stockholm, in 1924, to receive the Nobel Prize, and the speech he there delivered.

In *Yeats: The Man and the Masks* Richard Ellmann wrote of how the poet felt round about 1913:

Yet his house must somehow be put in order and he decided to write an autobiography. Lady Gregory had already started upon her memoirs of the early days of the Irish theatre, and Katharine Tynan had published her Twenty-Five Years: Reminiscences *in 1913, with several dozen of Yeats' early letters included without his permission. More important, George Moore had published* Hail and Farewell, *his mischievous reminiscences of the Irish literary movement. The book intermixed praise and blame for Yeats so cleverly that at first he did not take offence, but slowly it dawned on him that Moore had subtly made his whole movement ridiculous. At the end of* Responsibilities *(1914) Yeats placed a poem which expressed his feelings about Moore though without mentioning his name. What did Moore know of the mystical basis of the theatre, of the spiritual qualities of Yeats' life and writings? The poem ended:*

. . . all my priceless things
Are but a post the passing dogs defile.

But he did not stop at rejoinder. He would issue his own memoirs as an apologia, both for himself and for his family. The book, written in 1914, and published in 1915, under the title of Reveries Over Childhood and Youth, *is full of recollections of his mother's half-legendary relatives, whom he celebrated also in the prefatory poem to* Responsibilities, *and in fragmentary pictures shows the young poet as timid and sensitive, a good deal dominated by his father, though Yeats was careful to say nothing that would hurt his father's feelings. The memoirs were human and uncontroversial, coming down to about his twentieth year. For a time he went no further because too many living people and too many intimate memories were involved in the rest of his youth . . .*

So, in 1914, Yeats began where, we are told, the Lord Himself began, in the beginning, with his *Reveries over Childhood and Youth* (p. 163). By a comical oddity the first memory, or vision, was from London, nor was it particularly happy.

From there we return to Dublin (p. 166). That the poet as a youth in Dublin city should not have been able to cross the Ha'penny Toll Bridge for lack of the ha'penny gives that odd structure an eternal interest. Let us hope that the Jesuits gave Hopkins a few coins to rattle when he went walking in the evening. The ha'penny is no longer necessary, and poets and paupers may cross at will.

You may view the bridge as it still is, or envision it as it might have been if the project had gone ahead to build a gallery across the mottled waist of Anna Livia and there to house the Lane pictures.

But at a time when the loss of sixpence would have embarrassed the young man for days, he walked into untold riches in encountering O'Leary, the Fenian, and his sister, Ellen, who was also devoted to poetry.

Then in *The Trembling of the Veil*, in Yeats' memories of those *Four Years* from 1887–1891, he mentions an even more momentous meeting (p. 171). It happened in London, at least according to Yeats' recollection.

From here to the end of these brief extracts from his prose, let the great man speak for himself. Like his father before him, and his brother beside him, he was always well able to do so.

One final word. At the end of his most moving notes on the death of John Millington Synge, Yeats wrote: 'A good writer should be so simple that he has no faults, only sins.'

From REVERIES OVER CHILDHOOD AND YOUTH

I

MY FIRST MEMORIES are fragmentary and isolated and contemporaneous, as though one remembered some first moments of the Seven Days. It seems as if time had not yet been created, for all thoughts are connected with emotion and place without sequence.

I remember sitting upon somebody's knee, looking out of an Irish window at a wall covered with cracked and falling plaster, but what wall I do not remember, and being told that some relation once lived there. I am looking out of a window in London. It is in Fitzroy Road. Some boys are playing in the road and among them a boy in uniform, a telegraph-boy perhaps. When I ask who the boy is, a servant tells me that he is going to blow the town up, and I go to sleep in terror.

After that come memories of Sligo, where I live with my grandparents. I am sitting on the ground looking at a mastless toy boat with the paint rubbed and scratched, and I say to myself in great melancholy, 'It is further away than it used to be,' and while I am saying it I am looking at a long scratch in the stern, for it is especially the scratch which is further away. Then one day at dinner my great-uncle, William Middleton, says, 'We should not make light of the troubles of children. They are worse than ours, because we can see the end of our trouble and they can never see any end,' and I feel grateful, for I know that I am very unhappy and have often said to myself, 'When you grow up, never talk as grown-up people do of the happiness of childhood.' I may have already had the night of misery when, having prayed for several days that I might die, I began to be afraid that I was dying and prayed that I might live. There was no reason for my unhappiness. Nobody was unkind, and my grandmother has still after so many years my gratitude and my reverence. The house was so big that there was always a room to hide in, and I had a red pony and a garden where I could wander, and there were two dogs to follow at my heels, one white with some black spots on his head and the other with long black hair all over him. I used to think about God and fancy that I was very wicked, and one day when I threw a stone and hit a duck in the yard by mischance and broke its wing, I was full of wonder when I was told that the duck would be cooked for dinner and that I should not be punished.

Some of my misery was loneliness and some of it fear of old William Pollexfen, my grandfather. He was never unkind, and I cannot remember that he ever spoke harshly to me, but it was the custom to fear and admire him. He had won the freedom of some Spanish city, for saving life perhaps, but was so silent that his wife never knew it till he was near eighty, and then from the chance visit of an old sailor. She asked him if it was true and he said it was true, but she knew him too well to question and his old shipmate had left the town. She too had the habit of fear. We knew that he had been in many parts of the world, for there was a great scar on his hand made by a whaling-hook, and in the dining-room was a cabinet with bits of coral in it and a jar of water from the Jordan for the baptizing of his children and Chinese pictures upon rice-paper and an ivory walking-stick from India that came to me after his death. He had great physical strength and had the reputation of never ordering a man to do anything he would not do himself. He owned many sailing-ships and once, when a captain just come to anchor at Rosses Point reported something wrong with the rudder, had sent a message to say, 'Send a man down to find out what's wrong.' 'The crew all refuse' was the answer, and to that my grand-father answered, 'Go down yourself,' and not being obeyed, he dived from the main deck, all the neighbourhood lined along the pebbles of the shore. He came up with his skin torn but well informed about the rudder. He had a violent temper and kept a hatchet at his bedside for burglars and would knock a man down instead of going to law, and I once saw him hunt a party of men with a horsewhip. He had no relation, for he was an only child, and, being solitary and silent, he had few friends. He corresponded with Campbell of Islay who had befriended him and his crew after a shipwreck, and Captain Webb, the first man who had swum the Channel and who was drowned swimming the Niagara Rapids, had been a mate in his employ and a close friend. That is all the friends I can remember, and yet he was so looked up to and admired that when he returned from taking the waters of Bath his men would light bonfires along the railway lines for miles; while his partner, William Middleton, whose father after the great famine had attended the sick for weeks, and taken cholera from a man he carried in his arms into his own house and died of it, and was himself civil to everybody and a cleverer man than my grandfather, came and went without notice. I think I confused my grandfather with God, for I remember in one of my attacks of melancholy praying that he might punish me for my sins, and I was shocked and astonished when a daring little girl – a cousin, I think – having waited under a group of trees in the avenue, where she knew he would pass near four o'clock on the way to his dinner, said to him, 'If I were you and you were a little girl, I would give you a doll.'

Yet for all my admiration and alarm, neither I nor any one else thought it wrong to outwit his violence or his rigour; and his lack of suspicion and something helpless about him made that easy while it stirred our affection. When I must have been still a very little boy, seven or eight years old perhaps, an uncle called me out of bed one night, to ride the five or six miles to Rosses Point to borrow a railway-pass from a cousin. My grandfather had one, but thought it dishonest to let another use it, but the cousin was not so particular. I was let out through a gate that opened upon a little lane beside the garden away from earshot of the house, and rode delighted through the moonlight, and awoke my cousin in the small hours by tapping on his window with a whip. I was home again by two or three in the morning and found the coachman waiting in the little lane. My grandfather would not have thought such an adventure possible, for every night at eight he believed that the stable-yard was locked, and he knew that he was brought the key. Some servant had once got into trouble at night and so he had arranged that they should all be locked in. He never knew, what everybody else in the house knew, that for all the ceremonious bringing of the key the gate was never locked.

Even to-day when I read *King Lear* his image is always before me, and I often wonder if the delight in passionate men in my plays and in my poetry is more than his memory. He must have been ignorant, though I could not judge him in my childhood, for he had run away to sea when a boy, 'gone to sea through the hawse-hole' as he phrased it, and I can but remember him with two books – his Bible and Falconer's *Shipwreck*, a little green-covered book that lay always upon his table; he belonged to some younger branch of an old Cornish family. His father had been in the Army, had retired to become an owner of sailing-ships, and an engraving of some old family place my grandfather thought should have been his hung next a painted coat of arms in the little back parlour. His mother had been a Wexford woman, and there was a tradition that his family had been linked with Ireland for generations and once had their share in the old Spanish trade with Galway. He had a good deal of pride and disliked his neighbours, whereas his wife, a Middleton, was gentle and patient and did many charities in the little back parlour among frieze coats and shawled heads, and every night when she saw him asleep went the round of the house alone with a candle to make certain there was no burglar in danger of the hatchet. She was a true lover of her garden, and before the care of her house had grown upon her, would choose some favourite among her flowers and copy it upon rice-paper. I saw some of her handiwork the other day and I wondered at the delicacy of form and colour and at a handling that may have needed a magnifying-glass it was so minute. I can remember no other pictures but the Chinese paintings, and some coloured prints of battles in the Crimea upon the wall of a passage, and the painting of a ship at the passage end darkened by time.

My grown-up uncles and aunts, my grandfather's many sons and daughters, came and went, and almost all they said or did has faded from my memory, except a few harsh words that convince me by a vividness out of proportion to their harshness that all were habitually kind and considerate. The youngest of my uncles was stout and humorous and had a tongue of leather over the keyhole of his door to keep the draught out, and another whose bedroom was at the end of a long stone passage had a model turret-ship in a glass case. He was a clever man and had designed the Sligo quays, but was now going mad and inventing a vessel of war that could not be sunk, his pamphlet explained, because of a hull of solid wood. Only six months ago my sister awoke dreaming that she held a wingless sea-bird in her arms and presently she heard that he had died in his madhouse, for a sea-bird is the omen that announces the death or danger of a Pollexfen. An uncle, George Pollexfen, afterwards astrologer and mystic, and my dear friend, came but seldom from Ballina, once to a race-meeting with two postilions dressed in green; and there was that younger uncle who had sent me for the railway-pass. He was my grandmother's favourite, and had, the servants told me, been sent away from school for taking a crowbar to a bully.

I can only remember my grandfather punishing me once. I was playing in the kitchen and a servant in horseplay pulled my shirt out of my trousers in front just as my grandmother came in, and I, accused of I knew not what childish indecency, was given my dinner in a room by myself. But I was always afraid of my uncles and aunts, and once the uncle who had taken the crowbar to the bully found me eating lunch which my grandmother had given me and reproved me for it and made me ashamed. We break-fasted at nine and dined at four and it was considered self-indulgent to eat anything between meals; and once an aunt told me that I had reined in my pony and struck it at the same moment that I might show it off as I rode through the town, and I, because I had been accused of what I thought a very dark crime, had a night of misery. Indeed I remember little of childhood but its pain. I have grown happier with every year of life as though gradually conquering something in myself, for certainly my miseries were not made by others but were a part of my own mind.

From REVERIES OVER CHILDHOOD AND YOUTH

II

I HAD VERY LITTLE MONEY and one day the toll-taker at the metal bridge over the Liffey and a gossip of his laughed when I refused the halfpenny and said, 'No, I will go round by O'Connell Bridge.' When I called for the first time at a house in Leinster Road several middle-aged women were playing cards and suggested my taking a hand and gave me a glass of sherry. The sherry went to my head and I was impoverished for days by the loss of sixpence. My hostess was Ellen O'Leary, who kept house for her brother John O'Leary, the Fenian, the handsomest old man I had ever seen. He had been con-demned to twenty years' penal servitude but had been set free after five on condition that he did not return to Ireland for fifteen years. He had said to the Government, 'I will not return if Germany makes war on you, but I will return if France does.' He and his old sister lived exactly opposite the Orange leader, for whom he had a great respect. His sister stirred my affection at first for no better reason than her likeness of face and figure to the matron of my London school, a friendly person, but when I came to know her I found sister and brother alike were of Plutarch's people. She told me of her brother's life, of the foundation of the Fenian movement, and of the arrests that followed (I believe that her own sweetheart had somehow fallen among the wreckage), of sentences of death pronounced upon false evidence amid a public panic, and told it all without bitterness. No fanaticism could thrive amid such gentleness. She never found it hard to believe that an opponent had as high a motive as her own, and needed upon her difficult road no spur of hate.

Her brother seemed very unlike on a first hearing, for he had some violent oaths, 'Good God in Heaven' being one of them; and if he disliked anything one said or did, he spoke all his thought, but in a little one heard his justice match her charity. 'Never has there been a cause so bad', he would say, 'that it has not been defended by good men for good reasons.' Nor would he overvalue any man because they shared opinions; and when he lent me the poems of Davis and the Young Irelanders, of whom I had known nothing, he did not, although the poems of Davis had made him a patriot, claim that they were very good poetry.

He had the moral genius that moves all young people and moves them the more if they are repelled by those who have strict opinions and yet have lived commonplace lives. I had begun, as would any other of my training, to say violent and paradoxical things to shock provincial sobriety, and Dowden's ironical calm had come to seem but a professional pose. But here was something as spontaneous as the life of an artist. Sometimes he would say things that would have sounded well in some heroic Elizabethan play. It became my delight to rouse him to these outbursts, for I was the poet in the presence of his theme. Once when I was defending an Irish politician who had made a great outcry because he was treated as a common felon, by showing that he did it for the cause's sake, he said, 'There are things that a man must not do to save a nation.' He would speak a sentence like that in ignorance of its passionate value, and would forget it the moment after.

I met at his house friends of later life, Katharine Tynan, who still lived upon her father's farm, and Dr Hyde, still a college student who took snuff like those Mayo countrypeople whose stories and songs he was writing down. One constant caller looked at me with much hostility – jealous of my favour in O'Leary's eyes perhaps, though later on he found solider reason for hostility – John F. Taylor, an obscure great orator. The other day in Dublin I overheard a man murmuring to another one of his speeches as I might some Elizabethan lyric that is in my very bones. It was delivered at some Dublin debate, some College society perhaps. The Lord Chancellor had spoken with balanced unemotional sentences, now self-complacent, now derisive. Taylor began, hesitating and stopping for words, but after speaking very badly for a little, straightened his figure and spoke as out of a dream: 'I am carried to another age, a nobler society, and another Lord Chancellor is speaking. I am at the Court of the first Pharaoh.' Thereupon he put into the mouth of that Egyptian all his audience had listened to, but now it was spoken to the children of Israel. 'If you have any spirituality as you boast, why not use our great empire to spread it through the world, why still cling to that beggarly nationality of yours? What are its history and its works weighed with those of Egypt?' Then his voice changed and sank: 'I see a man at the edge of the crowd; he is standing listening there, but he will not obey'; and then with his voice rising to a cry, 'had he obeyed he would never have come down the mountain carrying in his arms the Tables of the Law in the language of the outlaw.'

I braved Taylor again and again as one might a savage animal as a test of courage, but always found him worse than my expectation. I would say, quoting Mill, 'Oratory is heard, poetry is overheard.' And he would answer, his voice full of contempt, that there was always an audience; and yet, in his moments of lofty speech, he himself was alone no matter what the crowd.

At other times his science or his Catholic orthodoxy, I never could discover which, would become enraged with my supernaturalism. I can but once remember escaping him unabashed and unconquered. I said with deliberate exaggeration at some evening party at O'Leary's, 'Five out of every six people have seen a ghost'; and Taylor fell into my net with, 'Well, I will ask everybody here.' I managed that the first answer should come from a man who had heard a voice he believed to be that of his dead brother, and the second from a doctor's wife who had lived in a haunted house and met a man with his throat cut, whose throat as he drifted along the garden-walk 'had opened and closed like the mouth of a fish'. Taylor threw up his head like an angry horse, but asked no further question, and did not return to the subject that evening. If he had gone on he would have heard from everybody some like story though not all at first hand, and Miss O'Leary would have told him what happened at the death of one of the MacManus brothers, well known in the politics of Young Ireland. One brother was watching by the bed where the other lay dying and saw a strange hawk-like bird fly through the open window and alight upon the breast of the dying man. He did not dare to drive it away and it remained there, as it seemed, looking into his brother's eyes until death came, and then it flew out of the window. I think, though I am not sure, that she had the story from the watcher himself.

With O'Leary Taylor was always, even when they differed, as they often did, gentle and deferential, but once only, and that was years afterwards, did I think that he was about to include me among his friends. We met by chance in a London street and he stopped me with an abrupt movement: 'Yeats,' he said, 'I have been thinking. If you and . . .' (naming another aversion) 'were born in a small Italian principality in the Middle Ages, he would have friends at Court and you would be in exile with a price on your head.' He went off without another word, and the next time we met he was no less offensive than before. He, imprisoned in himself, and not the always unperturbed O'Leary comes before me as the tragic figure of my youth. The same passion for all moral and physical splendour that drew him to O'Leary would make him beg leave to wear, for some few days, a friend's ring or pin, and gave him a heart that every pretty woman set on fire. I doubt if he was happy in his loves; for those his powerful intellect had fascinated were, I believe, repelled by his coarse red hair, his gaunt ungainly body, his stiff movements as of a Dutch doll, his badly rolled, shabby umbrella. And yet with women, as with O'Leary, he was gentle, deferential, almost diffident.

A Young Ireland Society met in the lecture-hall of a workmen's club in York Street with O'Leary for president, and there four or five university students and myself and occasionally Taylor spoke on Irish history or literature. When Taylor spoke, it was a great event, and his delivery in the course of a speech or lecture of some political verse by Thomas Davis gave me a conviction of how great might be the effect of verse, spoken by a man almost rhythm-drunk, at some moment of intensity, the apex of long-mounting thought. Verses that seemed when one saw them upon the page flat and empty caught from that voice, whose beauty was half in its harsh strangeness, nobility and style. My father had always read verse with an equal intensity and a greater subtlety, but this art was public and his private, and it is Taylor's voice that has rung in my ears and awakens my longing when I have heard some player speak lines, 'so naturally', as a famous player said to me, 'that nobody can find out that it is verse at all'. I made a good many speeches, more, I believe, as a training for self-possession than from desire of speech.

Once our debates roused a passion that came to the newspapers and the streets. There was an excitable man who had fought for the Pope against the Italian patriots and who always rode a white horse in our Nationalist processions. He got on badly with O'Leary, who had told him that 'attempting to oppress others was a poor preparation for liberating your own country'. O'Leary had written some letter to the Press condemning the 'Irish-American Dynamite Party', as it was called, and defining the limits of 'honourable warfare'. At the next meeting, the papal soldier rose in the middle of the discussion on some other matter and moved a vote of censure on

O'Leary. 'I myself', he said, 'do not approve of bombs, but I do not think that any Irishman should be discouraged.' O'Leary ruled him out of order. He refused to obey and remained standing. Those round him began to threaten. He swung the chair he had been sitting on round his head and defied everybody. However, he was seized from all sides and thrown out, and a special meeting called to expel him. He wrote letters to the papers and addressed a crowd somewhere. 'No Young Ireland Society', he pro-tested, 'could expel a man whose grandfather had been hanged in 1798.' When the night of the special meeting came his expulsion was moved, but before the vote could be taken an excited man announced that there was a crowd in the street, that the papal soldier was making a speech, that in a moment we should be attacked. Three or four of us ran and put our backs to the door while others carried on the debate. It was an inner door with narrow glass windows at each side and through these we could see the street-door and the crowd in the street. Presently a man asked us through the crack in the door if we would as a favour 'leave the crowd to the workmen's club upstairs'. In a couple of minutes there was a great noise of sticks and broken glass, and after that our landlord came to find out who was to pay for the hall-lamp.

From these debates, from O'Leary's conversation, and from the Irish books he lent or gave me has come all I have set my hand to since. I had begun to know a great deal about the Irish poets who had written in English. I read with excitement books I should find unreadable to-day, and found romance in lives that had neither wit nor adventure. I did not deceive myself; I knew how often they wrote a cold and abstract language, and yet I who had never wanted to see the houses where Keats and Shelley lived would ask everybody what sort of place Inchedony was, because Callanan had named after it a bad poem in the manner of *Childe Harold*. Walking home from a debate, I remember saying to some college student, 'Ireland cannot put from her the habits learned from her old military civilization and from a Church that prays in Latin. Those popular poets have not touched her heart, her poetry when it comes will be distinguished and lonely.' O'Leary had once said to me, 'Neither Ireland nor England knows the good from the bad in any art, but Ireland unlike England does not hate the good when it is pointed out to her.' I began to plot and scheme how one might seal with the right image the soft wax before it began to harden. I had noticed that Irish Catholics among whom had been born so many political martyrs had not the good taste, the household courtesy and decency of the Protestant Ireland I had known, yet Protestant Ireland seemed to think of nothing but getting on in the world. I thought we might bring the halves together if we had a national literature that made Ireland beautiful in the memory, and yet had been freed from provincialism by an exacting criticism, a European pose.

From FOUR YEARS: 1887–1891

PRESENTLY A HANSOM drove up to our door at Bedford Park with Miss Maud Gonne, who brought an introduction to my father from old John O'Leary, the Fenian leader. She vexed my father by praise of war, war for its own sake, not as the creator of certain virtues but as if there were some virtue in excitement itself. I supported her against my father, which vexed him the more, though he might have understood that, apart from the fact that Carolus Duran and Bastien-Lepage were somehow involved, a man young as I could not have differed from a woman so beautiful and so young. To-day, with her great height and the unchangeable lineaments of her form, she looks the Sibyl I would have had played by Florence Farr, but in that day she seemed a classical impersonation of the Spring, the Virgilian commendation 'She walks like a goddess' made for her alone. Her complexion was luminous, like that of apple-blossom through which the light falls, and I remember her standing that first day by a great heap of such blossoms in the window. In the next few years I saw her always when she passed to and fro between Dublin and Paris, surrounded, no matter how rapid her journey and how brief her stay at either end of it, by cages full of birds, canaries, finches of all kinds, dogs, a parrot, and once a full-grown hawk from Donegal. Once when I saw her to her railway carriage I noticed how the cages obstructed racks and cushions and wondered what her fellow-travellers would say, but the carriage remained empty. It was years before I could see into the mind that lay hidden under so much beauty and so much energy.

From IRELAND AFTER PARNELL

WHEN CARLETON was dying in 1869, he said there would be nothing more about Irish literature for twenty years, and his words were fulfilled, for the land war had filled Ireland with its bitterness; but imagination had begun to stir again. I had the same confidence in the future that Lady Gregory and I had eight or nine years later, when we founded an Irish Theatre, though there were neither, as it seemed, plays nor players. There were already a few known men to start my popular series, and to keep it popular until the men whose names I did not know had learnt to express themselves. I had met Dr Douglas Hyde when I lived in Dublin, and he was still an undergraduate. I have a memory of meeting in college rooms for the first time a very dark young man, who filled me with surprise, partly because he had pushed a snuffbox towards me, and partly because there was something about his vague serious eyes, as in his high cheek-bones, that suggested a different civilization, a different race. I had set him down as a peasant, and wondered what brought him to college, and to a Protestant college, but somebody explained that he belonged to some branch of the Hydes of Castle Hyde, and that he had a Protestant Rector for father. He had much frequented the company of old countrymen, and had so acquired the Irish language and his taste for snuff, and for moderate quantities of a detestable species of illegal whiskey distilled from the potato by certain of his neighbours. He had already – though intellectual Dublin knew nothing of it – considerable popularity as a Gaelic poet, mowers and reapers singing his songs from Donegal to Kerry. Years afterwards I was to stand at his side and listen to Galway mowers singing his Gaelic words without their knowing whose words they sang. It is so in India, where peasants sing the words of the great poet of Bengal without knowing whose words they sing, and it must often be so where the old imaginative folk-life is undisturbed, and it is so amongst schoolboys who hand their story-books to one another without looking at the title-page to read the author's name. Here and there, however, the peasants had not lost the habit of Gaelic criticism, picked up, perhaps, from the poets who took refuge among them after the ruin of the great Catholic families, from men like that O'Rahilly, who cries in a translation from the Gaelic that is itself a masterpiece of concentrated passion: –

The periwinkle and the tough dog-fish
Towards evening time have got into my dish.

An old rascal was kept in food and whiskey for a fortnight by some Connacht village under the belief that he was 'Craoibhin Aoibhin', 'the pleasant little branch', as Dr Hyde signed himself in the newspapers where the villagers had found his songs. The impostor's thirst only strengthened belief in his genius, for the Gaelic song-writers have had the infirmities of Robert Burns; 'It is not the drink but the company,' one of the last has sung. Since that first meeting Dr Hyde and I had corresponded, and he had sent me in manuscript the best tale in my *Fairy and Folk Tales*, and I think I had something to do with the London publication of his *Beside the Fire*, a book written in the beautiful English of Connacht, which is Gaelic in idiom and Tudor in vocabu-lary, and, indeed, the first book to use it in the expression of emotion and romance, for Carleton and his school had turned it into farce. Henley had praised him, and York Powell had said, 'If he goes on as he has begun, he will be the greatest folklorist who has ever lived'; and I know no first book of verse of our time that is at once so romantic and so concrete as his Gaelic *Abhla de'n Craoibh*; but in a few years Dublin was to laugh him, or rail him, out of his genius. He had no critical capacity, having indeed for certain years the uncritical folk-genius, as no educated Irishman or Englishman has ever had it, writing out of an imitative sympathy like that of a child catching a tune and leaving it to chance to call the tune; and the failure of our first attempt to create a modern Irish literature permitted the ruin of that genius. He was to create a popular movement, far more important in its practical results than any movement I could have made, no matter what my luck, but, being neither quarrelsome nor vain, he will not be angry if I say – for the sake of those who come after us – that I mourn for the 'greatest folklorist who ever lived', and for the great poet who died in his youth. The Harps and Pepperpots got him and the Harps and Pepperpots kept him till he wrote in our common English – 'It must be either English or Irish', said some patriotic editor, Young Ireland practice in his head – that needs such sifting that he who would write it vigorously must write it like a learned language, and took for his model the newspaper upon his breakfast-table, and became for no base reason beloved by multitudes who should never have heard his name till their schoolmasters showed it upon his tomb. That very incapacity for criticism made him the cajoler of crowds, and of individual men and women; 'He should not be in the world at all,' said one admiring elderly woman, 'or doing the world's work'; and for certain years young Irish women were to display his pseudonym 'Craoibhin Aoibhin', in gilt letters upon their hat-bands.

Dear Craoibhin Aoibhin, … impart to us –
We'll keep the secret – a new trick to please;
Is there a bridle for this Proteus
That turns and changes like his draughty seas,
Or is there none, most popular of men,
But when they mock us, that we mock again?

Standish O'Grady, upon the other hand, was at once all passion and all judgment. And yet those who knew him better than I assured me he could find quarrel in a straw; and I did know that he had quarrelled a few years back with Jack Nettleship. Nettleship's account had been: 'My mother cannot endure the God of the Old Testament, but likes Jesus Christ; whereas I like the God of the Old Testament, and cannot endure Jesus Christ; and we have got into the way of quarrelling about it at lunch; and once, when O'Grady lunched with us, he said it was the most disgraceful spectacle he had ever seen, and walked out.' Indeed, I wanted him among my writers because of his quarrels, for, having much passion and little rancour, the more he quarrelled, the nobler, the more patched with metaphor, the more musical his style became, and if he were in his turn attacked, he knew a trick of speech that made us murmur, 'We do it wrong, being so majestical, to offer it the show of violence.' Sometimes he quarrelled most where he loved most. A Unionist in politics, a leader-writer on the *Daily Express*, the most Conservative paper in Ireland, hater of every form of democracy, he had given all his heart to the smaller Irish landowners, to whom he belonged, and with whom his childhood had been spent, and for them he wrote his books, and would soon rage over their failings in certain famous passages that many men would repeat to themselves like poets' rhymes. All round us people talked or wrote for victory's sake, and were hated for their victories – but here was a man whose rage was a swan-song over all that he had held most dear, and to whom for that very reason every Irish imaginative writer owed a portion of his soul. In his unfinished *History of Ireland* he had made the old Irish heroes, Finn, and Oisin, and Cuchulain, alive again, taking them, for I think he knew no Gaelic, from the dry pages of O'Curry and his school, and condensing and arranging, as he thought Homer would have arranged and condensed. Lady Gregory has told the same tales, but keeping closer to the Gaelic text, and with greater powers of arrangement and a more original style, but O'Grady was the first, and we had read him in our teens. I think that, had I succeeded, a popular audience could have changed him little, and that his genius would have stayed as it had been shaped by his youth in some provincial society, and that to the end he would have shown his best in occasional thrusts and parries. But I do think that if, instead of that one admirable little book *The Bog of Stars*, we had got all his histories and imaginative works into the hands of our young men, he might have brought the imagination of Ireland nearer the Image and the honeycomb.

From HODOS CHAMELIONTOS

WHEN STAYING with Hyde in Roscommon, I had driven over to Lough Key, hoping to find some local memory of the old story of Tumaus Costello, which I was turning into a story now called *Proud Costello, Macdermot's Daughter, and the Bitter Tongue*. I was rowed up the lake that I might find the island where he died; I had to find it from Hyde's account in the *Love-Songs of Connacht*, for when I asked the boatman, he told the story of Hero and Leander, putting Hero's house on one island, and Leander's on another. Presently we stopped to eat our sandwiches at the 'Castle Rock', an island all castle. It was not an old castle, being but the invention of some romantic man, seventy or eighty years ago. The last man who had lived there had been Dr Hyde's father, and he had but stayed a fortnight. The Gaelic-speaking men in the district were accustomed, instead of calling some specially useless thing a 'white elephant', to call it 'The Castle on the Rock'.

The roof was, however, still sound, and the windows unbroken. The situation in the centre of the lake, that has little wood-grown islands, and is surrounded by wood-grown hills, is romantic, and at one end, and perhaps at the other too, there is a stone platform where meditative persons might pace to and fro. I planned a mystical Order which should buy or hire the castle, and keep it as a place where its members could retire for a while for contemplation, and where we might establish mysteries like those of Eleusis and Samothrace; and for ten years to come my most impassioned thought was a vain attempt to find philosophy and to create ritual for that Order. I had an unshakable conviction, arising how or whence I cannot tell, that invisible gates would open as they opened for Blake, as they opened for Swedenborg, as they opened for Boehme, and that this philo-sophy would find its manuals of devotion in all imaginative literature, and set before Irishmen for special manual an Irish literature which, though made by many minds, would seem the work of a single mind, and turn our places of beauty or legendary association into holy symbols. I did not think this philosophy would be altogether pagan, for it was plain that its symbols must be selected from all those things that had moved men most during many, mainly Christian, centuries.

I thought that for a time I could rhyme of love, calling it *The Rose*, because of the Rose's double meaning; of a fisherman who had 'never a crack' in his heart; of an old woman complaining of the idleness of the young, or of some cheerful fiddler, all those things that 'popular poets' write of, but that I must some day – on that day when the gates began to open – become difficult or obscure. With a rhythm that still echoed Morris I prayed to the Red Rose, to Intellectual Beauty: –

Come near, come near, come near – Ah, leave me still
A little space for the rose-breath to fill!
Lest I no more hear common things . . .
But seek alone to hear the strange things said
By God to the bright hearts of those long dead,
And learn to chaunt a tongue men do not know.

I do not remember what I meant by 'the bright hearts', but a little later I wrote of spirits 'with mirrors in their hearts'.

My rituals were not to be made deliberately, like a poem, but all got by that method Mathers had explained to me, and with this hope I plunged without a clue into a labyrinth of images, into that labyrinth that we are warned against in those *Oracles* which antiquity has attributed to Zoroaster, but modern scholarship to some Alexan-drian poet: 'Stoop not down to the darkly splendid world wherein lieth continually a faithless depth and Hades wrapped in cloud, delighting in unintelligible images.'

From THE TRAGIC GENERATION

I AM CERTAIN of one date, for I have gone to much trouble to get it right. I met John Synge for the first time in the autumn of 1896, when I was one-and-thirty, and he four-and-twenty. I was at the Hôtel Corneille instead of my usual lodging, and why I cannot remember, for I thought it expensive. Synge's biographer says that you boarded there for a pound a week, but I was accustomed to cook my own breakfast, and dine at an Anarchist restaurant in the Boulevard St Jacques for little over a shilling. Some one, whose name I forget, told me there was a poor Irishman at the top of the house, and presently introduced us. Synge had come lately from Italy, and had played his fiddle to peasants in the Black Forest — six months of travel upon fifty pounds — and was now reading French literature and writing morbid and melancholy verse. He told me that he had learned Irish at Trinity College, so I urged him to go to the Aran Islands and find a life that had never been expressed in literature, instead of a life where all had been expressed. I did not divine his genius, but I felt he needed something to take him out of his morbidity and melancholy. Perhaps I would have given the same advice to any young Irish writer who knew Irish, for I had been that summer upon Inishmaan and Inishmore, and was full of the subject. My friends and I had landed from a fishing-boat to find ourselves among a group of islanders, one of whom said he would bring us to the oldest man upon Inishmaan. This old man, speaking very slowly, but with laughing eyes, had said, 'If any gentleman has done a crime, we'll hide him. There was a gentleman that killed his father, and I had him in my house for six months till he got away to America.'

From that on I saw much of Synge, and brought him to Maud Gonne's, under whose persuasion, perhaps, he joined the 'Young Ireland Society of Paris', the name we gave to half a dozen Parisian Irish, but resigned after a few months because 'it wanted to stir up Continental nations against England, and England will never give us freedom until she feels she is safe', the one political sentence I ever heard him speak. Over a year was to pass before he took my advice and settled for a while in an Aran cottage, and became happy, having escaped at last, as he wrote, 'from the squalor of the poor and the nullity of the rich'. I almost forget the prose and verse he showed me in Paris, though I read it all through again when after his death I decided, at his written request, what was to be published and what not. Indeed, I have but a vague impression, as of a man trying to look out of a window and blurring all that he sees by breathing upon the window. According to my Lunar parable, he was a man of the twenty-third Phase; a man whose subjective lives — for a constant return to our life is a part of my dream — were over; who must not pursue an image, but fly from it, all that subjective dreaming, that had once been power and joy, now corrupting within him. He had to take the first plunge into the world beyond himself, the first plunge away from himself that is always pure technique, the delight in doing, not because one would or should, but merely because one can do.

He once said to me, 'A man has to bring up his family and be as virtuous as is compatible with so doing, and if he does more than that he is a puritan; a dramatist has to express his subject and to find as much beauty as is compatible with that, and if he does more he is an aesthete,' that is to say, he was consciously objective. Whenever he tried to write drama without dialect he wrote badly, and he made several attempts, because only through dialect could he escape self-expression, see all that he did from without, allow his intellect to judge the images of his mind as if they had been created by some other mind. His objectivity was, however, technical only, for in those images paraded all the desires of his heart. He was timid, too shy for general conversation, an invalid and full of moral scruple, and he was to create now some ranting braggadocio, now some tipsy hag full of poetical speech, and now some young man or girl full of the most abounding health. He never spoke an unkind word, had admirable manners, and yet his art was to fill the streets with rioters, and to bring upon his dearest friends enemies that may last their lifetime.

No mind can engender till divided into two, but that of a Keats or a Shelley falls into an intellectual part that follows, and a hidden emotional flying image, whereas in a mind like that of Synge the emotional part is deadened and stagnant, while the intellectual part is a clear mirror-like technical achievement.

But in writing of Synge I have run far ahead, for in 1896 he was but one picture among many. I am often astonished when I think that we can meet unmoved some person, or pass some house, that in later years is to bear a chief part in our life. Should there not be some flutter of the nerve or stopping of the heart like that MacGregor Mathers experienced at the first meeting with a phantom?

Many pictures come before me without date or order. I am walking somewhere near Luxembourg Gardens when Synge, who seldom generalizes and only after much thought, says, 'There are three things any two of which have often come together but never all three: ecstasy, asceticism, austerity; I wish to bring all three together'.

I notice that MacGregor Mathers considers William Sharp vague and sentimental, while Sharp is repelled by Mathers' hardness and arrogance. William Sharp met Mathers in the Louvre, and said, 'No doubt considering your studies you live upon milk and fruit.' And Mathers replied, 'No, not exactly milk and fruit, but very nearly so'; and now Sharp has lunched with Mathers and been given nothing but brandy and radishes.

Mathers is much troubled by ladies who seek spiritual advice, and one has called to ask his help against phantoms who have the appearance of decayed corpses, and try to get into bed with her at night. He has driven her away with one furious sentence, 'Very bad taste on both sides.'

I take hashish with some followers of the eighteenth-century mystic Saint-Martin. At one in the morning, while we are talking wildly, and some are dancing, there is a tap at the shuttered window; we open it and three ladies enter, the wife of a man of letters who thought to find no one but a confederate, and her husband's two young sisters whom she has brought secretly to some disreputable dance. She is very confused at seeing us, but as she looks from one to another understands that we have taken some drug and laughs; caught in our dream we know vaguely that she is scandalous according to our code and to all codes, but smile at her benevolently and laugh.

I am at Stuart Merrill's, and I meet there a young Jewish Persian scholar. He has a large gold ring, seemingly very rough, made by some amateur, and he shows me that it has shaped itself to his finger, and says, 'That is because it contains no alloy — it is alchemical gold.' I ask who made the gold, and he says a certain Rabbi, and begins to talk of the Rabbi's miracles. We do not question him — perhaps it is true — perhaps he has imagined it all — we are inclined to accept every historical belief once more.

I am sitting in a café with two French-Americans, a German poet, Dauthendey, and a silent man whom I discover to be Strindberg, and who is looking for the Philosophers' Stone. One French-American reads out a manifesto he is about to issue to the Latin Quarter; it proposes to establish a communistic colony of artists in Virginia, and there is a footnote to explain why he selects Virginia: 'Art has never flourished twice in the same place. Art has never flourished in Virginia.'

Dauthendey, who has some reputation as a poet, explains that his poems are without verbs, as the verb is the root of all evil in the world. He wishes for an art where all things are immovable, as though the clouds should be made of marble. I turn over the page of one of his books which he shows me, and find there a poem in dramatic form, but when I ask if he hopes to have it played he says: 'It could only be played by actors before a black marble wall, with masks in their hands. They must not wear the masks, for that would not express my scorn for reality.'

I go to the first performance of Alfred Jarry's *Ubu Roi*, at the Théâtre de L'Oeuvre, with the Rhymer who had been so attractive to the girl in the bicycling costume. The audience shake their fists at one another, and the Rhymer whispers to me, 'There are often duels after these performances,' and he explains to me what is happening on the stage. The players are supposed to be dolls, toys, marionettes, and now they are all hopping like wooden frogs, and I can see for myself that the chief personage, who is some kind of King, carries for sceptre a brush of the kind that we use to clean a closet. Feeling bound to support the most spirited party, we have shouted for the play, but that night at the Hôtel Corneille I am very sad, for comedy, objectivity, has displayed its growing power once more. I say: 'After Stéphane Mallarmé, after Paul Verlaine, after Gustave Moreau, after Puvis de Chavannes, after our own verse, after all our subtle colour and nervous rhythm, after the faint mixed tints of Conder, what more is possible? After us the Savage God.'

From DRAMATIS PERSONAE

I

WHEN I WAS THIRTY YEARS OLD the three great demesnes of three Galway houses, Coole House, Tulira Castle, Roxborough House, lay within a half-hour or two hours' walk of each other. They were so old they seemed unchanging; now all have been divided among small farmers, their great ancient trees cut down. Roxborough House was burnt down during the Civil War; Coole House has passed to the Forestry Department; but Tulira Castle is inhabited by blood relatives of those who built it. I went there for the first time with Arthur Symons, then editor of the *Savoy* magazine. I was taking him here and there through Ireland. We had just been sight-seeing in Sligo. Edward Martyn, met in London, perhaps with George Moore, had seemed so heavy, uncouth, countrified that I said as we turned in at the gate: 'We shall be waited on by a barefooted servant.' I was recalling a house seen at Sligo when a child. Then I saw the great trees, then the grey wall of the Castle.

Edward Martyn brought us up the wide stairs of his Gothic hall decorated by Crace and showed us our rooms. 'You can take your choice,' he said. I took out a penny to toss, shocking Symons, who was perhaps all the more impressed by his surroundings because of what I had said about bare feet. I think the man of letters has powers of make-believe denied to the painter or the architect. We both knew that those pillars, that stair and varnished roof with their mechanical ornament, were among the worst inventions of the Gothic revival, but upon several evenings we asked Edward Martyn to extinguish all light except that of a little Roman lamp, sat there in the shadows, as though upon a stage set for *Parsifal*. Edward Martyn sat at his harmonium, so placed among the pillars that it seemed some ancient instrument, and played Palestrina. He hated that house in all its detail – it had been built by his mother when he was a very young man to replace some plain eighteenth-century house – all except an ancient tower where he had his study. A fire had destroyed the old house, and whatever old furniture or pictures the family possessed, as though fate had deliberately prepared for an abstract mind that would see nothing in life but its vulgarity and temptations. In the tower room, in a light filtered through small stained-glass windows, without any quality of design, made before Whall rediscovered the methods of mediaeval glass-workers, he had read Saint Chrysostom, Ibsen, Swift, because they made abstinence easy by making life hateful in his eyes. He drank little, ate enormously, but thought himself an ascetic because he had but one meal a day, and suffered, though a courteous man, from a subconscious hatred of women. His father had been extravagantly amorous; I was later to collect folk-lore from one of his father's peasant mistresses, then an old woman. I have heard of his getting from his horse to chase a girl for a kiss. Edward's mother, who still lived, and is a frail, pinched figure in my memory, had tried to marry him to women who did not share or even understand his tastes and were perhaps chosen for that reason. Edward, who admired Beardsley for his saturnine genius, had commissioned from him a great stained-glass window for the hall. And had Beardsley lived another year, his fat women, his effeminate men, his children drawn so as to suggest the foetus, would have fed Edward's hatred of life. I can remember his mother's current selection, a pretty somewhat ruddy girl, saying: 'I never could stand those Beardsleys,' fixing her eye on an incomparable Utamaro. The drawing-room furniture was vulgar and pretentious, because he thought himself bound to satisfy what he believed to be the taste of women. Only his monklike bedroom, built over the stables and opening into the tower on the opposite side to the house, his study in the tower, and the pictures, showed his own improving taste. His first purchase, a large coffee-coloured sea picture by Edwin Ellis – not my friend the Blake scholar, but the Academician – had been a mistake; then, perhaps under the influence of George Moore, a relative on his father's side came Degas, Monet, Corot, Utamaro, and of these pictures he talked with more intelligence, more feeling than when he talked of literature. His Degas showed the strongly marked shoulder-blades of a dancing-girl, robbing her of voluptuous charm. Degas had said to him: 'Cynicism is the only sublimity.' It hung somewhere near the Utamaro, which pleased him because of its almost abstract pattern, or because the beautiful women portrayed do not stir our Western senses.

When Symons and I paid our visit, Martyn had just finished *The Heather Field*. Alexander had praised it and refused it, and he talked of having it produced in Germany. He sat down daily to some task, perhaps *Maeve*, but I was certain even then, I think, that though he would find subjects, construct plots, he would never learn to write; his mind was a fleshless skeleton. I used to think that two traditions met and destroyed each other in his blood, creating the sterility of a mule. His father's family was old and honoured; his mother but one generation from the peasant. Her father, an estate steward, earned money in some way that I have forgotten. His religion was a peasant religion; he knew nothing of those interpretations, casuistries, whereby my Catholic acquaintance adapt their ancient rules to modern necessities. What drove him to those long prayers, those long meditations, that stern Church music? What secret torture?

III

Presently, perhaps after Arthur Symons had gone, Lady Gregory called, reminded me that we had met in London though but for a few minutes at some fashionable house. A glimpse of a long vista of trees, over an undergrowth of clipped laurels, seen for a moment as the outside car approached her house on my first visit, is a vivid memory. Coole House, though it has lost the great park full of ancient trees, is still set in the midst of a thick wood, which spreads out behind the house in two directions, in one along that edges of a lake which, as there is no escape for its water except a narrow subterranean passage, doubles or trebles its size in winter. In later years I was to know the edges of that lake better than any spot on earth, to know it in all the changes of the seasons, to find there always some new beauty. Wondering at myself, I remember that when I first saw that house I was so full of the mediaevalism of William Morris that I did not like the gold frames, some deep and full of ornament, round the pictures in the drawing-room; years were to pass before I came to understand the earlier nineteenth and later eighteenth century, and to love that house more than all other houses. Every generation had left its memorial; every generation had been highly educated; eldest sons had gone the grand tour, returning with statues or pictures; Mogul or Persian paintings had been brought from the Far East by a Gregory chairman of the East India Company, great earthenware ewers and basins, great silver bowls, by Lady Gregory's husband, a famous Governor of Ceylon, who had married in old age, and was now some seven years dead; but of all those Gregorys, the least distinguished, judged by accepted standards, most roused my interest — a Richard who at the close of the eighteenth century was a popular brilliant officer in the Guards. He was accused of pleading ill-health to escape active service, and though exonerated by some official inquiry, resigned his commission, gave up London and his friends. He made the acquaintance of a schoolgirl, carried her off, put her into a little house in Coole demesne, afterwards the steward's house, where she lived disguised as a boy until his father died. They married, and at the end of last century the people still kept the memory of her kindness and her charity. One of the latest planted of the woods bore her name, and is, I hope, still called, now that the Government Foresters are in possession, 'The Isabella Wood'. While compelled to live in boy's clothes she had called herself 'Jack the Sailor' from a song of Dibdin's. Richard had brought in bullock-carts through Italy the marble copy of the Venus de' Medici in the drawing-room, added to the library the Greek and Roman Classics bound by famous French and English binders, substituted for the old straight avenue two great sweeping avenues each a mile or a little more in length. Was it he or his father who had possessed the Arab horses, painted by Stubbs? It was perhaps Lady Gregory's husband, a Trustee of the English National Gallery, who had bought the greater number of the pictures. Those that I keep most in memory are a Canaletto, a Guardi, a Zurbarán. Two or three that once hung there had, before I saw those great rooms, gone to the National Gallery, and the fine portraits by Augustus John and Charles Shannon were still to come. The mezzotints and engravings of the masters and friends of the old Gregorys that hung round the small downstairs breakfast-room, Pitt Fox, Lord Wellesley, Palmerston, Gladstone, many that I have forgotton, had increased generation by generation, and amongst them Lady Gregory had hung a letter from Burke to the Gregory that was chairman of the East India Company saying that he committed to his care, now that he himself had grown old, the people of India. In the hall, or at one's right hand as one ascended the stairs, hung Persian helmets, Indian shields, Indian swords in elaborate sheaths, stuffed birds from various parts of the world, shot by whom nobody could remember, portraits of the members of Grillion's Club, illuminated addresses presented in Ceylon or Galway, signed photographs or engravings of Tenny-son, Mark Twain, Browning, Thackeray, at a later date paintings of Galway scenery by Sir Richard Burton, bequeathed at his death, and etchings by Augustus John. I can remember somebody saying: 'Balzac would have given twenty pages to the stairs.' The house itself was plain and box-like, except on the side towards the lake, where somebody, probably Richard Gregory, had enlarged the drawing-room and dining-room with great bow windows. Edward Martyn's burnt house had been like it doubtless, for it was into such houses men moved, when it was safe to leave their castles, or the thatched cottages under castle walls; architecture did not return until the cut stone Georgian houses of a later date.

IV

Lady Gregory, as I first knew her, was a plainly dressed woman of forty-five, without obvious good looks, except the charm that comes from strength, intelligence and kindness. One who knew her at an earlier date speaks of dark skin, of an extreme vitality, and a portrait by Mrs Jopling that may have flattered shows considerable beauty. When her husband died, she had given up her London house, had devoted herself to the estate and to her son, spending little that mortgages might be paid off. The house had become her passion. That passion grew greater still when the house took its place in the public life of Ireland. She was a type that only the superficial observer could identify with Victorian earnestness, for her point of view was founded, not on any narrow modern habit, but upon her sense of great literature, upon her own strange feudal, almost mediaeval youth. She was a Persse — a form of the name Shakespeare calls Percy — descended from some Duke of Northumberland; her family had settled in the seventeenth century somewhere in the midlands, but finding, the legend declares, the visits of Lord Clanricarde, going and returning between his estate and Dublin, expensive, they had moved that they might be no longer near the high road and bought vast tracts of Galway land. Roxborough House, small and plain, but interesting for its high-pitched roof — the first slate roof built in Galway — was beside the road from Gort to Loughrea, a few yards from the bounding wall of a demesne that was nine miles round. Three or four masons were, during Lady Gregory's girlhood, continually busy upon the wall. On the other side of the road rose the Slievoughter range, feeding grouse and wild deer. The house contained neither pictures nor furniture of historic interest. The Persses had been soldiers, farmers, riders to hounds and, in the time of the Irish Parliament, politicians; a bridge within the wall commemorated the victory of the Irish Volunteers in 1782, but all had lacked intellectual curiosity until the downfall of their class had all but come. In the latter half of the nineteenth century Lady Gregory was born, an older and a younger sister gave birth to Sir Hugh Lane and to that John Shawe-Taylor who, by an act of daring I must presently describe, made the settlement of the Land Question possible.

Popular legend attributes to all the sons of the house daring and physical strength; some years ago, Free State Ministers were fond of recounting the adventures of Lady Gregory's 'Seven Brothers', who, no matter who objected to their rents, or coveted their possessions, were safe 'because had one been killed, the others would have run down and shot the assassin'; how the wildest of the brothers, excluded by some misdemeanour from a Hunt Ball, had turned a hose on the guests; how, a famous shot, he had walked into a public-house in a time of disturbance and put a bullet through every number on the clock. They had all the necessities of life on the mountain, or within the walls of their demesne, exporting great quantities of game, ruling their tenants, as had their fathers before, with a despotic benevolence, were admired, and perhaps loved, for the Irish people, however lawless, respect a rule founded upon some visible supremacy. I heard an old man say once to Lady Gregory: 'There was never a man that could hold a bow with your brothers.' Those brothers were figures from the eighteenth century. Sir Jonah Barrington might have celebrated their lives, but their mother and the mother of John Shawe-Taylor were of the nineteenth in one of their characteristics. Like so many Irish women of the upper classes, who reacted against the licence, the religious lassitude of the immediate past, they were evangelical Protestants, and set out to convert their neighbourhood. Few remember how much of this movement was a genuine enthusiasm; that one of its missionaries who travelled Ireland has written her life, has described meetings in peasant cottages where everybody engaged in religious discussion, has said that she was everywhere opposed and slandered by the powerful and the wealthy because upon the side of the poor. I can turn from the pages of her book with sympathy. Were I a better man and a more ignorant I had liked just such a life. But that missionary would have met with no sympathy at Roxborough, except, it may be, amongst those boisterous brothers or from one studious girl, for Roxborough Protestantism was on the side of wealth and power. All there had an instinctive love for their country or their neighbourhood, the mail-boat had not yet drawn the thoughts of the wealthy classes elsewhere. My great-grandmother Corbet, the mistress of Sandymount Castle, had been out of Ireland but once. She had visited her son, afterwards Governor of Penang, at his English school, carrying a fortnight's provisions, so great were the hazards of the crossing; but that was some two generations earlier. Their proselytism expressed their love, they gave what they thought best. But the born student of the great literature of the world cannot proselytize, and Augusta Persse, as Lady Gregory was then named, walked and discussed Shakespeare with a man but little steadier than her brothers, a scholar of Trinity, in later years a famous botanist, a friendship ended by her alarmed mother. Was it earlier or later that she established a little shop upon the estate and herself sold there that she might compel the shopkeepers to bring down their exorbitant prices? Other well-born women of that time, Ruskin's Rose amongst them, did the same. Born in 1852, she had passed her formative years in comparative peace, Fenianism a far-off threat; and her marriage with Sir William Gregory in her twenty-ninth year, visits to Ceylon, India, London, Rome, set her beyond the reach of the bitter struggle between landlord and tenant of the late 'seventies and early 'eighties. She knew Ireland always in its permanent relationships, associations – violence but a brief interruption – never lost her sense of feudal responsibility, not of duty as the word is generally understood, but of burdens laid upon her by her station and her character, a choice constantly renewed in solitude. 'She has been', said an old man to me, 'like a serving-maid among us. She is plain and simple, like the Mother of God, and that was the greatest lady that ever lived.' When in later years her literary style became in my ears the best written by woman, she had made the people a part of her soul; a phrase of Aristotle's had become her motto: 'To think like a wise man, but to express oneself like the common people.'

V

When I went to Coole the curtain had fallen upon the first act of my drama. In 1891 I had founded in London the Irish Literary Society, joined by most London journalists of Irish birth, a couple of years later in Dublin, the National Literary Society; these societies had given, as I intended, opportunity to a new generation of critics and writers to denounce the propagandist verse and prose that had gone by the name of Irish literature, and to substitute for it certain neglected writers: Sir Samuel Ferguson, a writer of ballads dry in their eighteenth-century sincerity; Standish O'Grady, whose *History of Ireland* retold the Irish heroic tales in romantic Carlylean prose; the Clarence Mangan of the *Dark Rosaleen* and *O'Hussey's Ode to The Maguire*, our one poet raised to the first rank by intensity, and only that in these or perhaps in the second of these poems. No political purpose informed our meetings; no Lord Mayor, no Member of Parliament, was elected to the chair. John O'Leary, the old Fenian, since his return from his Parisian exile more scholar than politician, first president of the National Literary Society, was succeeded by Dr Douglas Hyde. His famous presidential lecture upon what he called 'The De-Anglicisation of Ireland' led to the foundation of the Gaelic League, which, though not yet the great movement it became, was soon stronger than the movement in English. Irishmen who wrote in the English language were read by the Irish in England, by the general public there, nothing was read in Ireland except newspapers, prayer-books, popular novels; but if Ireland would not read literature it might listen to it, for politics and the Church had created listeners. I wanted a Theatre – I had wanted it for years, but knowing no way of getting money for a start in Ireland, had talked to Florence Farr, that accomplished speaker of verse, less accomplished actress, of some little London hall, where I could produce plays. I first spoke to Lady Gregory of my abandoned plan for an Irish Theatre, if I can call anything so hopeless a plan, in the grounds of a little country house at Duras, on the sea-coast, where Galway ends and Clare begins. She had brought me to see the only person in Galway, perhaps I should say in Ireland, who was in any real sense her friend. His romantic name is written on the frame of a picture by Stott of Oldham in the Dublin Municipal Gallery: 'Given by A. Gregory and W. R. Gregory' – Lady Gregory's son, at the time of my first visit a boy of seventeen – 'in memory of Count Florimond de Basterot.' He was a Catholic, an old man crippled by the sins of his youth, much devoted to his prayers, but an accomplished man of the world.

He had flats in Paris and in Rome and divided his year between them and his little Galway house, passing through Dublin as quickly as possible because he thought it 'a shabby England'. Ancestors had fled from the French Revolution, bought a considerable Galway estate long since sold to some other landlord or divided among the tenants. In a few years, seven or eight, he was to speak to Lady Gregory and to myself, and for the first time, of estate and house, to drive us through what had once been park, show where the walls had stood, what had been garden, an aviary in the midst of it, where the avenue had wound, where upon that avenue he, a boy in his teens, and his father's men-servants had thrown a barricade across it and stood with guns in their hands. His father had died in debt, and at that time a creditor could seize a body and prevent its burial until paid. The creditor arrived, but at the sight of armed men fled. De Basterot fulfilled a saying I have heard somewhere: 'Things reveal themselves passing away.' We never saw him again. In five or six weeks, several men and women with old French titles announced upon a black-edged card the death of 'Florimond, Alfred Jacques, Comte de Basterot, Cheva-lier de l'Ordre du Saint Sépulcre, leur Cousin Germain et Cousin'. In his garden under his friendly eyes, the Irish National Theatre, though not under that name, was born. I may then have used for the first time the comparison which in later years I turned into a proverb. Except during certain summer months, when they roost in the fields, crows at nightfall return to the vast rookeries round Tulira Castle, whirling, counter-whirling, clamorous; excited, as it seems, by the sublime dance. It was the one unforgettable event of my first visit as of other visits there. And I was accustomed to say to Lady Gregory when it seemed that some play of mine must be first performed outside Ireland, or when it seemed, as it did once or twice, that I myself might find it impossible to live in Ireland: 'The crows of Tulira return to their trees in winter' or 'The crows return at nightfall,' meaning that, after my death, my books would be a part of Irish literature. She, however, with her feeling for immediate action, for the present moment, disapproved of my London project. She offered to collect or give the money for the first Irish performances. My *Countess Cathleen* was ready, and either I or Lady Gregory spoke to Edward Martyn, who gave up a proposed German performance and became enthusiastic. Then came an unexpected difficulty. Dublin had two theatres, the Royal and the Gaiety, that had been granted patents, a system obsolete everywhere else. No performance, except for charity, could be given but at these two theatres; they were booked for the best months of the year by English travelling companies and in the worst months were expensive. We had to change the law, which we did with the assistance of an old friend of Lady Gregory's husband, Lecky the historian, representative in Parliament of Trinity College. The writing of letters, talks in the Lobby of the House of Commons, seemed to take up all our time.

INDEX

INDEX OF FIRST LINES

PICTURE CREDITS

*By courtesy of: The Directors of the Abbey Theatre, Dublin, photo Rex
Roberts: 49, 115. Liam Blake/Slide File, Dublin: frontispiece. Bord Failte,
Dublin: 30–1, 66–7, 102, 120. Central Bank of Ireland, Dublin: 51.
The Cuala Press, Dublin – illustrations by T. Sturge Moore from
Reveries over Childhood and Youth: 26, 160; illustration by Elinor
Monsell from Responsibilities: 60; illustration by Jack B. Yeats for cover of
On the Boiler: 132; illustration by Edmund Dulac from Last Poems and
Two Plays: 140; The Ballad Seller by Jack B. Yeats: 138. Hulton
Picture Company: 72, 73, 111. Imperial War Museum, London: 90. Hugh
Lane Municipal Gallery of Modern Art, Dublin: 34, 55, 69, 71, 74–5,
78–9, 82, 106–7, 131. Mansell Collection, London: 36–7, 95 (above).
National Gallery of Ireland, Dublin: 7, 23, 29, 35, 38–9, 42–3, 58–9,
63, 84, 118, 122. National Library of Ireland, Dublin: 20–1, 24, 52, 70
(below), 96–7, 129. National Museum of Ireland, Dublin: 33. Popperfoto,
London: 93. Private Collection/photo Pyms Gallery, London: 46–7. Pyms
Gallery, London: 138. Slide File, Dublin: 10–11. Sligo County Museum:
94–5. Edwin Smith: 57, 89, 137. Colin Smythe: 40, 81, 87, 99, 121.*

*The publishers wish to thank Anne Yeats and Michael B. Yeats for
permission to reproduce the illustrations by W.B. Yeats, Jack B. Yeats and John
B. Yeats, as well as illustrations from The Cuala Press, family photographs
and the costume designs by Charles Ricketts.*